SEAN O'CASEY:
THE MAN AND HIS PLAYS

Other Books by Jules Koslow

SEAN O'CASEY
The Man and His Plays

by Jules Koslow

The Citadel Press
New York

for SUE

CONTENTS

ACKNOWLEDGMENTS

The author is grateful to the late Sean O'Casey for his help and encouragement during the writing of this book. He also wishes to thank Macmillan & Co. Ltd., London; The Macmillan Company, New York; and St. Martin's Press, New York, for permission to quote from Mr. O'Casey's works.

INTRODUCTION

One of the most important aspects of Sean O'Casey's plays, if not the most important, is his genius for viewing and expressing in dramatic form the political and social scene of our day.

Joseph M. Hone writes that "his plays are sociological representations, an intelligent exploitation of the external features of life which has attracted his rich powers of observation..."

Michael Macliammoir, in a speech, "Problem Plays," remarks that O'Casey's plays deal so definitely with social conditions that what he has to say on just one social problem, for instance, housing, "could with advantage be read to the Dail and the Dublin Corporation... before every sitting."

John W. Cunliffe defines the central motivating force in O'Casey's characters as one in which political ideas conflict with adverse material conditions:

"In the clash between the splendour of their political ideals and the squalor of their material surroundings he saw a dramatic irony as moving to tears and laughter as a Greek protagonist's struggles against fate or a romantic hero's overwhelming by circumstance and some inner flaw."

The political and social affairs of our age rather than the

personal crises of individuals form the core of O'Casey's dramas. As Ronald Peacock observes:

"A private crisis has little significance for a public eye dazzled by revolution and international vicissitudes. The 'tragic hero' has in consequence disappeared. The tragic plays of O'Casey are symptomatic of this situation. His characters, vivid as some of them are, are not as important as the larger political tragedy of which they are fortuitous victims."

O'Casey's plays fall easily into the definition which he himself propounded: "A play must not be the commonplace portrayal of the trivial events in the life of this man or that woman, but a commentary of life itself."

From the remarks of critics, and especially from an analysis of his plays, there is sufficient justification for a study based, in the main, on the political and social aspects of the dramas. Therefore, this criticism will be limited to an analysis of these facets of his plays and will dwell upon factors such as style, characterization, language, only as they bear upon the central aim of the study.

The plays will be examined in chronological order. This method allows for a logical unfolding of O'Casey's growth and widening interests, from his Irish national period, through his transition period, to the world outlook of his later plays, and, at the sunset of his life, his return home to Ireland and her people.

JULES KOSLOW

New York
1966

SEAN O'CASEY:
THE MAN AND HIS PLAYS

one

INTO THE LIGHT OF THE LIVING

Sean O'Casey, the youngest child of a family of seven, was born in Dublin in 1880 in one of the fine old eighteenth century Georgian mansions that had become by then "gaunt houses ... sad remnants of past ages ... slum tenements crowded with poverty-stricken inhabitants ..." His mother, Sue, a courageous and noble working-class woman, who had buried two other Johnnys, children who had fought and lost the battle against disease arising out of poverty, nursed him, petted him and pushed him out of the dark shadows into the light of the living.

O'Casey, in his autobiography, refers to his health in his early childhood thus: "Delicately and physically undecided, he crept along." He states that his mother "nursed him viciously" through his childhood illnesses. A form of ulcerated eyeballs made him almost blind. Again, it was his mother who came to his aid.

"Only his mother harassed her mind for help; only she, with deep pity and unbreakable patience, stood between him and the chance that his sight might go, leaving him helpless in the hands of man and no nearer to God; only she raised the banner of fear for him in the face of everyone she met, pried everywhere for assistance to save him from the evil of perpetual darkness."

Thus, plagued by poverty and general poor health, he passed his childhood on the streets of Dublin. His education was meager. A Protestant clergyman finally dragged the half-blind boy off the streets into the schoolroom. O'Casey bitterly remarks about "...being lugged along at the backside of this soft-hatted stiff-collared egg-headed oul' henchman of heaven, to be added to his swarm of urchins cowering and groping about in the rag-and-bone education provided by the church and state for children of those who hadn't the wherewithal to do anything better."

His school life was cut short violently, when, after the schoolmaster had given him a sound beating, he retaliated by bringing "an ebony ruler down on the pink, baldy, hoary oul' head of hoary oul' Slogan."

Out in the world, lacking a formal education, he joined the ranks of the unskilled workers. Errand-boy, newspaper-sorter, dockworker, hod-carrier, stone-breaker on the roads and janitor were to be but some of the numerous jobs he was to hold until his "knock-on-the-door" of literature would be heard, and he could put away the tools of the worker and take up the tools of the writer.

All was not labor for young O'Casey, for he needed the rose as well as the loaf, and soon he began to be interested in affairs around him. From three directions the call came to him—the church, socialism, the Gaelic League. Each voice spoke to him in its own way, summoning him to its particular fold; each call, in certain respects, tempted him out of the darkness and into the light of hope.

"Three appeals to him, the humblest Roman of them all; for God, for Man, and for Country; three so different from each other, yet all alike in so far that each was made in the dimness, silently, and in fear...The call to freedom from sin, freedom from employers, freedom from national oppression..."

After a brief period as an active member of the church, he joined the Gaelic League, mastered Irish, and was soon so enthusiastic about the cause that his fellow-workingmen began to call him "Irish Jack." But after a fairly long period of activity, his interest in the Gaelic League began to flag (although his interest in the Gaelic language continued) when his day-to-day life and struggles among the working people directed his interest to his own class. He joined the Irish Transport and General Workers Union when he became convinced that there was a need for "a new song and a new hope..."

During the Transport Workers Strike of 1913 he worked closely with Jim Larkin, the famous union leader. O'Casey was appointed head of a committee to raise funds for shoes and clothing for the children and wives of striking workers. O'Casey himself, very poorly clothed and often without a few pence in his pocket for "a bit of bread and a cup of tay," his health extremely poor, continued with his organizational work, but constantly seeing before him "a thick, black sky full of the pale dead faces of workers, life but faintly sketched in each of them, like white, wan moons looking down on a broken purple star falling phut-long out of their own presunctified horrorizon."

O'Casey severed his relations with the Gaelic League because he did not agree with those who, as he states in *The Story of the Irish Citizen Army*, "no doubt, preferred Caithlin ni Houlihan in a respectable dress than a Caithlin in the garb of a working woman."

The embittered strike of 1913 resulted in the formation of the Citizen Army, with Jim Larkin and later Jim Connolly as the leader. O'Casey became the secretary of the Citizen Army and played an influential part in its organization and development. He formulated the Constitution of the Citizen Army; and this, with few revisions, remained the guiding body of principles for the organization. He broke with the Citizen Army before the Easter Week Uprising of 1916 over a dispute which arose around the Irish patriot Countess Markievicz.

But O'Casey was not completely absorbed by his organizational interests, as a reading of his first published book, *The Story of the Irish Citizen Army*, reveals. In the midst of his activities he had certain doubts, or, perhaps, certain higher feelings. For instance, he writes of attending a function of the Citizen Army at Croydon Park:

"Here, with one's head in the bosom of Nature, to what a small compass shrinks even the Constitution of the Irish Citizen Army! How horrible is a glistening, oily rifle to one of the tiny daisies, that cowers in a rosy sleep...giving to the world to which it has been born the fullest beauty and fragrance that its simple nature has to give."

A political prisoner in the hands of the British during the Easter Week Uprising, O'Casey did no fighting. However, he did have the highly uncomfortable experience of being lined up against a wall for execution. A scuffle at the other end of the street diverted the soldiers and permitted him to escape. As an observer, albeit a forced one, he was able to digest the dramatic events of that week more dispassionately than if he had been in the very thick of the fight, and later, his play, *The Plough and the Stars*, set against the background of the Easter Week Uprising, was deeply influenced by the position of O'Casey during this period.

Although O'Casey didn't learn how to read or write until he was about thirteen years of age, by the time he was seventeen he had made his first effort in the drama. A year later he had the disappointment of having one of his first plays, *Frost in the Flower*, rejected by a little theatre because it was highly satirical of the members of that group. He submitted the same play to the Abbey Theatre, and, although it was rejected, O'Casey received from the Abbey a critical evaluation of the play and encouragement to continue his playwrighting efforts. He submitted several more plays to the Abbey, all of which were politely but firmly rejected.

Contrary to popular belief, O'Casey did not learn playwrighting by watching plays at the Abbey Theatre. O'Casey himself reveals that he had been to the Abbey only three times before he wrote his first play and that he learned to write plays by reading and acting them out with his brother. It was not, however, until after the Rebellion of 1916 that O'Casey began to give most of his attention to writing instead of to politics.

Thus, it will be observed, O'Casey was a political rebel first, and then a poet, a participant in the Irish labor and independence movements long before his first play was produced. Although O'Casey had playwrighting ambitions while he was still a very young man, it was not until 1923-4, more than twenty years after his initial efforts, with the acceptance by the Abbey Theatre of his *The Shadow of a Gunman* and *Juno and the Paycock*, that his literary career was finally launched. The road

17

to recognition had been long and hard, and O'Casey himself admitted some years later, in an interview granted the press before the New York opening of his play, *Within the Gates,* that had the Abbey not accepted his plays in 1923, he was ready at that time to quit writing and revert to the toil of a common laborer.

His literary career was to be no less turbulent than his non-literary one. With the presentation of his third full-length drama by the Abbey Theatre, *The Plough and the Stars,* O'Casey became the target against which was hurled all the pent up bitterness and prejudice of people who had lived through the events described by O'Casey but refused or were ashamed to see themselves mirrored. Middle-class puritans, blown-up patriots, narrow clericals, jealous fellow writers and critics, outraged womanhood personified by the members of the Cumann na mBan, the Society of Women, condemned him, called him a slanderer and vilifier of national Irish life. The very doors of the Abbey Theatre were slammed in his face. And as O'Casey himself states: "He turned away . . . never after set a foot either on the Abbey stage or in the Abbey Green Room. He'd hoist his sail and go to England . . ."

In 1927, he left Ireland for England, left the land and the Abbey which it is true had given him much, but which, in return, had received much more. It was a self-imposed exile, an exile of a man who no longer could tolerate a "Kathleen, daughter of Houlihan now, untidy termagant, brawling out her prayers." He never returned, and with his actress wife, Eileen Reynolds, and family resided in England until his death on September 18, 1964.

In addition to the turbulent political and social movements

in which O'Casey was so active, certain literary influences were influential in shaping his outlook. His formal schooling being negligible he was forced to educate himself. He devoted much of his time and energy to studying Shakespeare, old Irish literature and Gaelic. As a youth, he was deeply influenced by Ruskin. Concerning the literary influences upon him when he was in his late twenties, O'Casey writes in his autobiography:

"Sean was now in bad company constantly. Not a week passed but he was found hobnobbing with Shaw, Darwin, Frazer, and France, and the volubility and loudness of their positive talk were having a dangerous effect upon him."

From this brief sketch of O'Casey's life, certain factors are of major importance: his environment, the slums of Dublin; his manner of making a living as an unskilled worker; his interest in Gaelic and the Irish movement for independence; his extreme poverty and ill health; his political ideology, veering further and further to the Left; his activities in the ranks of organized labor and the Irish Citizen Army; and his literary interests, running the gamut from Shakespeare to Shaw.

Certainly, whether or not O'Casey uttered a truism when he stated that "the main element in any play is the author," his own background and experiences play a vital role in the conception and execution of his literary works. In the course of our examination of his plays, we shall notice the close association between his own life and the characters and events in his dramas. For O'Casey, more than any other modern dramatist, exploited the events of his own life, his surroundings and the people he knew and observed. His use of real life material, selected, heightened and dramatized into dynamic stage action,

19

prompted George Jean Nathan, a great admirer of O'Casey, to remark that his plays have a "profundity of feeling, the real pity and sorrow and pain and joy, the true shooting beauty of life tragically experienced and life desperately lived...."

two

THE IRISH WAR PERIOD

The years 1916 to 1923 were years of terror and violence in Ireland. From the outbreak of the Easter Week Rebellion in 1916 to the final victory of the Free State government over the rebels in 1923, no peace of mind or safety of person was possible for the mass of Irish—Protestant or Catholic, Nationalist or Republican, worker or employer. The struggle for Irish independence, carried on for hundreds of years, was reaching its climax.

As in other struggles for independence, various leaders and movements, each claiming to be the voice and the way, issued manifestoes, armed their followers and broke the heads of those who disagreed with them. Disillusion, blind hatred and confusion, as well as idealism and heroism, were expressed in the speeches and actions of the innumerable factions participating in the struggle.

In the name of freedom and liberty Irish fought British, Free Stater fought Ulsterman, Protestant fought Catholic and Sinn Fein fought Sinn Fein. Organized armies, bands of gunmen and individual assassins roamed the land. The order of the day was curfews, military zones, martial law, executions, looting and expropriation of land and property.

Yet, through it all shone the high ideals of Wolfe Tone, Robert Emmet and Charles Parnell; through it all the magic word freedom inspired a nation that had suffered and sacrificed. Here was a people, after years of strife, on the threshold of destiny—the dams of common sense, restraint, tolerance were not strong enough to check the flood-tides of frenzied patriotism, unbridled excesses and intolerance.

It is in this setting that the three plays of Sean O'Casey's Irish national period are laid.

The action of *The Shadow of a Gunman*, produced in 1923, takes place in a Dublin tenement in the month of May, 1920. The Sinn Fein Terror and the Black and Tan Counter-Terror had made each passing day a day of apprehension and each night a night of death. Through the land the cry "Up the Republic" was echoed by rifle and pistol shots. Life was dangerous and death was not reserved for the aged and ailing. Seumas Shields, in the play, describes the condition of the land when he says:

"The country is gone mad. Instead of counting their beads now they're countin' bullets; their Hail Marys and paternosters are burstin' bombs—burstin' bombs, an' the rattle of machine guns; petrol is their holy water; their mass is a burnin' buildin'; their De Profundis is 'The Soldiers' Song,' an' their creed is, I believe in the gun almighty, maker of heaven an' earth—an' it's all for 'the glory o' God an' the honour o' Ireland.' "

The plot of the play revolves about this same Seumas, a peddler, and his friend Donal Davoren, a poet, and pretty Minnie Powell, a working girl. Davoren speaks so eloquently

22

of Irish independence that the other people in the house believe him to be a gunman on the run. Basically, he is weak and cowardly, but he is so pleased that he is considered a dangerous fellow that he does not deny it. A friend leaves a piece of luggage in the room, and Seumas and Donal discover too late that it contains bombs. The Black and Tans arrive, Minnie Powell takes the suitcase to her room, is discovered, and subsequently is killed on the way to headquarters when she tries to escape.

Upon hearing of Minnie's fate, the "heroes" are conscience-stricken, and Davoren cries:

"Ah me, alas! Pain, pain, pain ever, for ever! It's terrible to think that little Minnie is dead, but it's still more terrible to think that Davoren and Shields are alive! Oh, Donal Davoren, shame is your portion now till the silver cord is loosened and the golden bowl be broken. Oh, Davoren, Donal Davoren, poet and poltroon, poltroon and poet!"

Juno and the Paycock (1924), like his first play, has a tenement house setting. The action of the play takes place during the highly complex and confusing period around 1922 when the Irish Free State had been set up but had not succeeded in unifying the country around it. The Sinn Fein had split, and the bitter internecine struggle terrorized the country. Yet life had to go on, and *Juno* is not so much the story of the factional struggle (although important elements of it are woven into the play) as a delineation of the life of the Boyle family as it now humorously, and now tragically, pits itself against the demoralizing and disintegrating forces of poverty.

Against this background of civil war, we find the Boyle family, poor and down-at-the-heel, trying to eke out an existence. Juno

23

Boyle, a woman of forty-five, is the mother. O'Casey describes her thus:

"...twenty years ago...[she] must have been a pretty woman, but her face has now assumed that look which ultimately settles down upon the faces of the women of the working-class, a look of listless monotony and harassed anxiety, blending with an expression of mechanical resistance."

She tries courageously to keep her family together while her husband, "Captain" Boyle, the "paycock," is idling away his time with another wastrel, "Joxer" Daly.

When the play opens, Mary, the daughter, is out on strike, and Johnny, the son, who had been shot in the hip during Easter Week (and later loses his arm), is ill. An unexpected stroke of good fortune descends upon the family in the form of a supposed bequest, and the Boyles begin to buy articles on credit to refurnish their home: the "paycock" sports a new suit of clothes; a new gramophone is installed in the living room; Mary leaves Jerry Devine, a union organizer, and takes up with Charlie Bentham, a school teacher and aspiring lawyer.

But the bequest proves to be a mistake, and tragedy descends quickly upon the Boyle family: the creditors invade the apartment and strip it; Mary is abandoned by Charlie Bentham and discovers that she is pregnant; and Johnny, who has informed on a comrade, is taken away by two Irregulars, and executed.

Juno, with the wreckage of her family all about her, cries: "Sacred Heart o' Jesus, take away our hearts o' stone, and give us hearts o' flesh! Take away this murdherin' hate, an' give us Thine own eternal love!" The "paycock" lets fall on the floor the last sixpence he has in the world and exclaims: "The blinds is down, Joxer, the blinds is down!"

The play ends with Boyle, roaring drunk, sitting in the empty apartment with his drinking companion, "Joxer" Daly, and moaning his ineffectual complaint that the "whole world's in a terrible state of chassis!"

The third and last play of the Irish War Period is *The Plough and the Stars* (1926). The setting is in the Dublin slums during the Easter Week Rebellion of 1916. At this time, the defense arm of the labor movement (the Citizen Army) and the Sinn Fein military organization (the Irish Volunteers), after going their separate ways for some time, united their forces to challenge the rule of Britain.

The declaration of an "Irish Republic," the short but bloody battle in buildings and streets of Dublin and the defeat and execution of the Irish leaders are a matter of history. But it was necessary to delineate and portray, in addition to the story of the military participants, the situation of the overwhelming mass of Dubliners, who prayed, cursed, wept, worked, and, in general, tried to continue life amidst a revolutionary situation. What was the reaction of the wife whose husband was at the General Post Office, firing and being fired on by the British? What were the feelings of the loyalist surrounded by a sea of inflammatory patriotic utterances? What thoughts went through the mind and what feelings through the heart of a mother with a son fighting the Germans in France on the side of the British? What can be said of the men who uttered tons of verbiage in praise of Cathleen ni Houlihan but lacked an ounce of courage when they realized that her path was a thorny one? The Socialist, the Orangeite, the British Tommy, the patriot—what did they think, how did they act at the time of national emergency and personal danger? What, indeed, did

25

the whole situation mean in terms of material gain and ideological objectives? These are the questions that O'Casey raises
and attempts to answer in *The Plough and the Stars*.

The first act opens in November, 1915, and we are introduced to the various inhabitants of a tenement: Nora Clitheroe,
a young, sensitive wife; Jack Clitheroe, her husband, an officer
in the Citizen Army; the Young Covey, cousin to Jack, and
a Socialist; Peter Flynn, uncle to Nora, an excitable, fussy man;
Fluther Good, a loud-mouthed, hard-drinking carpenter; Bessie
Burgess, loyalist, whose son is fighting with the British in
France; Mrs. Gogan, a charwoman; and Mollser, her daughter,
a consumptive.

The second act takes place in a public-house, outside of
which a meeting is being held by the leaders of the independence movement. The words of the speaker (alleged to be the
actual words from the address in which Padraig Pearse proclaimed the Republic) drift into the pub:

"Comrade soldiers of the Irish Volunteers and of the Citizen
Army, we rejoice in this terrible war. The old heart of the
earth needed to be warmed with the red wine of the battle-
fields.... Such august homage was never offered to God as
this: the homage of millions of lives given gladly for love of
country."

But in the pub, Rosie, a prostitute, is complaining about the
lack of business since the men are at the meeting and "thinkin'
of higher things than a girl's garthers." The Young Covey,
filled with self-importance and socialist doctrines, sneers at the
aims of the kind of freedom, national liberation, proclaimed
by the speaker:

"Freedom! What's th' use o' freedom, if it's not economic

26

freedom? ... Look here, comrade, there's only one freedom for th' workin' man: conthrol o' th' means o' production, rates of exchange, an' th' means of disthribution."

Bessie Burgess, loyalist that she is, complains that she cannot understand how the Irish "... can call themselves Catholics, when they won't lift a finger to help poor little Catholic Belgium ... There's a storm of anger tossin' in me heart, thinkin' of all th' poor Tommies, an' with them me own son .., layin' down their white bodies, shredded into torn an' bloody pieces, on th' althar that God Himself has built for th' sacrifice of heroes!"

Mrs. Gogan threatens Bessie Burgess:

"Come on, now, me loyal lassie, dyin' with grief for little Catholic Belgium! When Jinnie Gogan's done with you, you'll have a little leisure lyin' down to think an' pray for your king an' counthry!"

The two women soon drop politics and switch to slandering each other's virtue; Rosie's honor is defended by Fluther when the Young Covey calls her a prostitute; Rosie rewards Fluther by accepting his invitation to "come on into th' snug, me little darlin', an' we'll have a few dhrinks before I see you home."

The plough and the stars are forgotten when there is drinking, fighting, quibbling and whoring to be done. Even at the end of the act, when Captain Brennan, Lieutenant Langon and Commander Clitheroe respectively cry: "Imprisonment for th' Independence of Ireland!" "Wounds for th' Independence of Ireland!" and "Death for th' Independence of Ireland!" their defiant utterances become lost as Rosie, hanging on the arm of Fluther, sings:

27

"I once had a lover, a tailor, but he could do nothin' for me,
An' then I fell in with a sailor as strong an' as wild as th' sea.
We cuddled an' kissed with devotion, till th' night from th'
    mornin' had fled;
An' there, to our joy, a bright bouncin' boy
Was dancin' a jig in th' bed!"

The third act takes place during the Easter Week Rebellion.
Nora, in a frenzy over the safety of her husband, has searched
the bullet-riddled streets for him in vain and is finally brought
back to the tenement by Fluther. Later, Jack does appear but
is deaf to the pleas of Nora to desert the struggle. He leaves
her to rejoin his comrades as she pitifully calls after him: "Oh,
Jack, I gave you everything you asked of me ... Don't fling me
from you, now!"

However, for the inhabitants of the tenement, the revolution, the ailing Mollser, political differences, and even personal
danger are forgotten when the word gets around that there is
looting going on nearby. Another army marches off, but this
time with baby carriages and hand carts to bring home the
spoils of non-participation. The act closes with Bessie Burgess
heroically volunteering to go through the streets of Dublin
to fetch a doctor for the completely distraught Nora Clitheroe.

The fourth act brings the play to a swift and tragic conclusion. Nora loses her mind, Jack Clitheroe is killed in action,
Mollser dies of consumption and Bessie Burgess is mortally
wounded by the Tommies. Fluther, Peter and the Young Covey
are taken into custody by the British as in the distance we
hear the booming of artillery, the rattle of machine gun fire and

the singing of a patriotic song by the rebels, and "Keep the Home Fires Burning" by the British.

From the brief summaries of these plays, we can see that the Irish War Period was the historical epoch in which all of O'Casey's early plays are set. The period acts as no mere atmospheric backdrop but is an integral part of the plays. This confusing, tragic and exciting era furnishes the stimulus, the perspective, the *sine qua non* for his dramas.

But O'Casey is a dramatist, not a historian. His function is not to give a scholarly presentation of the period, but instead, by means of the dramatic construction and theses of his plays, to integrate the period in such a manner that the audience or the reader can see and feel the era more clearly, and in emotional as well as intellectual terms.

It was not an easy matter for a patriotic Irishman (and O'Casey, in his own way, was a patriot) to picture his people in the throes of a life and death struggle in a dispassionate manner. Sides had been chosen, and we know from O'Casey's autobiography that he had definite opinions on the various situations that arose in his plays. Yet, his dramas are not partial to this or that side. Rather, they are a portrayal of life, a presentation of the viewpoint of many factions and individuals, and a description of people and events. His method is that of vivisection, cutting away the outer layer of skin, and with great skill selecting and revealing the formerly concealed organs. In this connection, Milton Waldman, reviewing *The Plough and the Stars* for the *London Mercury*, makes the following comment:

"Apparently he sees the sequence of revolutionary episodes as one vast drama, and from it selects for his own purposes

29

dramatic episodes which he places against a shrewdly observed background of proletarian life."

This selective process Horace Schipp describes as:

"... the method of presenting the comic, exuberantly romantic Irish lower class against the tragic background of the Irish revolution, of allowing the tragedy to sweep devastatingly into the lives of his characters, and of revealing the pitiful helplessness of individual men and women against the overwhelming forces of circumstances."

This realistic way of dealing with people involved in the Irish Revolution is a departure from the traditional way of presenting the Irish and their struggle for freedom. Padraic Colum makes an interesting point when he states that, "in the early days of the [Abbey] Theatre, warfare was an aspiration, not an experience."

Yeats, for instance, in *Cathleen ni Hoolihan*, has her remark: "They that had red cheeks will have pale cheeks for my sake; and for all that they will think they are well paid." O'Casey, on the other hand, has Juno say to Johnny: "Ah, you lost your best principle, me boy, when you lost your arm; them's the only sort o' principles that's any good to a workin' man."

Andrew E. Malone, in his remarks on *Juno*, sums up O'Casey's approach to the question of patriotism and sacrifice:

"Sacrifices are made in the name of, and for, the motherland, but the mother is sacrificed, derided, spurned, or ignored. Ireland is loved as an abstraction, a dream; Juno is compelled to live in a slum, to see her children sacrificed, but she is ignored because she is merely a reality of flesh and blood."

The human aspects of the struggle are rooted deeply in the

30

political and social conditions of the time. Desmond McCarthy, commenting on the political background of *Juno*, writes:

"It is, on its political side, a ruthless exposure of the feckless lack of public spirit which made the disaster possible; of a general lack of moral courage which, combined with an insanely romantic readiness to kill and be killed in a sprinkling of individuals, makes national life impossible."

This is but one view of O'Casey's use of the political scene in his plays. Starkie claims that O'Casey does not expose in order to preach a doctrine, but rather gives an honest portrayal of conditions and allows the chips to fall where they may:

"We must not consider Sean O'Casey a social dramatist like many of his contemporaries, who are eager to preach against this or that vice by means of thesis-drama; he simply looks around him and determines to omit none of the various and complex details that appear to him."

Thus, Starkie would classify O'Casey as a writer who tries to understand the world with his eye. Starkie's appraisal of O'Casey at this stage of his development seems to have great merit. After all, the plays themselves are based upon people O'Casey saw, events that he experienced, ideals that he shared. This view is shared by various critics, among whom is J. M. Hone, who states: "Mr. O'Casey has rendered with admirable art a reality of Ireland in troubled times ..." Another reviewer in *Theatre Arts Monthly* calls *Juno* "a shattering picture of what civil war means to the people that suffer it, of what life is like in the slums of Dublin, as of all great cities, of the great enigma of human suffering." Colum expresses the thought that O'Casey was writing from observation and experience: "O'Casey knew them [the young militarists] in the Citizen

31

Army; he saw what their fight for freedom and their interne-cine fight brought to the dwellers in the tenements, and he has set it all down."

O'Casey's use of the urban proletariat and life in the Dublin slums was a distinct departure from the existing drama of the time in Ireland. We look in vain in the plays of Lady Gregory, W. B. Yeats, J. M. Synge and others for the city worker or the Dublin slums. The proletariat of Dublin and the slums in which they lived were not considered to have dramatic value. We had to wait for a man who had lived, worked, suffered, laughed and loved amongst these people in this environment; we had to wait, in addition, for a man who had the literary genius to lift this material out of the natural setting and place it dramatically upon the stage. The Irish theatre found such a man in O'Casey. P. S. O'Hegarty writes:

"... Mr. O'Casey is significant in the evolution of the Irish dramatic movement. He breaks the long line of peasant dram-atists and peasant plays. He is the first modern Irish dramatist to come out of brick and mortar and write about brick and mortar."

An examination of the three plays discussed so far will reveal that out of a total of forty-six characters that appear on stage only three are not of proletarian background. Not one major character is of non-working-class stock, and the three who are alien to the slums are but a step or so removed from them— Mr. Mulligan, the petty landlord in The Shadow of a Gunman, Charlie Bentham, the poor school teacher in Juno, and A Woman, the frightened creature who appears for several mo-ments in The Plough and the Stars.

Except for the tavern scene in The Plough and the Stars

O'Casey never strays away from the tenement buildings themselves. Even in that scene, it will be observed, the tavern is
a working-class tavern frequented by slum-dwellers. It is not
until the appearance of *The Silver Tassie*, five years after the
presentation of O'Casey's first play, that he ventures to leave
the slums and to use another setting.

O'Casey did not glorify his slum-dwellers. This is a fault
which a playwright with less vision and genius than O'Casey
could have easily committed. His heart and hand were with
the people with whom he had been raised. Yet an examination
of his plays reveals that in spite of his sympathy for them,
like Chekhov, he had the intellectual honesty to portray his
people with all their faults. His was a clinical portrait of his
people, and if among them there were cowards like Donal
Davoren, wastrels like "Captain" Jack Boyle, drunkards like
Fluther Good, and whores like Rosie Redmond, he had the
honesty and integrity to put them before an audience and to
suffer the consequences of being called a traitor to his class
and country. He could have romanticized his characters, allowed them to swoon at the mention of Cathleen ni Hoolihan
instead of swilling when the great moments of Irish history
were unfolding before their very eyes.

He reaped the consequences of his realism in the riots that
occurred during the opening performances of *The Plough and
the Stars*. A few excerpts from accounts of these riots will give
a picture of the reactions of the audience to his play.

The *Daily Telegraph* of March 11, 1926, reports:

"A dozen screaming women rushing from the pit and climb-
ing on the stage. A fierce and penetrating argument with the
actors upon the merits of Morality, Patriotism, and the Virtues

33

of Home Life. An attempt by a wild young man to pull down the curtain, followed by the sudden and precipitant descent over the footlights of that identical young man on the point of some-body's fist. Speeches from the gallery upon Death and Glory and the Immortality of the Soul. And the subsequent arrival of the police in force to restore order and to rescue Art from Demos."

John W. Cunliffe in his book, *Modern English Playwrights*, reports that a young man in the audience stood up and shouted: "We fought in Easter Week and we don't want any more of this play. It is slander on the Citizen's Army."

O'Casey himself gives the best eyewitness account of the riots in his autobiography. After refusing Yeats' request that the police be called so that the play might go on, O'Casey finally, though reluctantly, agreed.

"The police were summoned, and the play began again—two, in fact: one on the stage and the other in the auditorium. Yeats tore down the stairs, and rushed on to the stage to hold the fort till the constables came. The whole place became a mass of moving, roaring people, and Yeats roared louder than any of them. Rowdy, clenching, but well-groomed hands reached up to drag down the fading black and gold front curtain; others, snarling curiously, tried to tug up the very chairs from their roots in the auditorium; while some, in frenzy, pushed at the stout walls to force them down. Steamy fumes ascended here and there in the theatre, and a sickly stench crept all over the place, turning healthy-looking faces pale. The high, hysterical, distorted voices of women kept squealing that Irish girls were noted over the whole world for their modesty, and that Ireland's name was holy; that the Republican flag had

34

never seen the inside of a public-house; that this slander of the Irish race would mean the end of the Abbey Theatre; and that Ireland was Ireland through joy and through tears. Up in the balcony, a section was busily bawling out *The Soldier's Song*, while a tall fellow frantically beat time on the balcony-rail with a walking-stick. Barry Fitzgerald became a genuine Fluther Good, and fought as Fluther himself would fight, sending an enemy, who had climbed on to the stage, flying into the stalls with a flutherian punch on the jaw. And in the midst of the fume, the fighting, the stench, the shouting, Yeats, as mad as the maddest there, pranced on the stage, shouting out his scorn, his contempt; his anger making him like unto an aged Cuchullin in his hero-rage; his long hair waving, he stormed in utter disregard of all around him, confronting all those who cursed and cried out shame and vengeance on the theatre, as he conjured up a vision for them of O'Casey on a cloud, with Fluther on his right hand and Rosie Redmond on his left, rising upwards to Olympus to get from the waiting gods and goddesses a triumphant apotheosis for a work well done in the name of Ireland and of art.

"Then the constables flooded into the theatre, just in time. Rough and ready, lusty guardians of the peace. They filed into the theatre as Irish constables for the first time in their life; mystified, maybe, at anyone kicking up a row over a mere play. They pulled the disturbers out, they pushed them out, and, in one or two instances, carried them out, shedding them like peas from the pod of the theatre, leaving them in the cold street outside to tell their troubles to their neighbours or to the stars. Then the play went on, halting often, and agitated to its end."

William Butler Yeats, in his speech to the audience, summed up the effect of the riot when he said:

"I thought you have got tired of this. It commenced fifteen years ago. You have disgraced yourselves again. Is this to be an ever recurring celebration of the arrival of Irish genius? Once more you have rocked the cradle of genius. The news of what is happening here will go from country to country. You have once more rocked the cradle of reputation. The fame of O'Casey is born tonight. This is apotheosis."

The Dublin slums were among the worst in Europe. Colum writes that there were "40,000 families in single rooms" and as many as "84 children living in one house."

O'Casey writes: "Rotten Dublin; lousy Dublin, what had it for anyone? What had it for him? Poverty and pain and penance. They were its three castles. The gates of Dublin: poverty, pain, and penance." But if O'Casey is bitter about Dublin, it is because he loves the people in it and hates to see them bruised and beaten down by poverty, disease and hardship.

Throughout his plays we see the effects of slum life upon its inhabitants. A great and noble creature like Juno, a woman of sufficient proportions to be the symbol of Mother in all lands, a woman of depth, understanding and courage, is rewarded for all of her virtues by the destruction of her home and the disintegration of her family. Little Mollser, a victim of slum-life, dies of consumption; Minnie Powell, grasping out for romance and excitement amidst the drabness of her surrounding, is killed; Nora, who wants love and a home, is rewarded with misery and madness. Even the "paycock" is a good man at heart, gay and likable, but has been consumed by the cancer of idleness, penny-pinching and lack of self-respect—all of which can be traced to the poverty and wretchedness of his life.

A discussion of the slum-people in O'Casey's plays would not be complete without some mention of the positive virtues that he portrays in his characters. O'Casey gives us a full picture, not a naturalistic display of sordidness. His tenement house inhabitants are courageous (Minnie), expansive (Juno), and willing to extend a helping hand when a neighbour is in trouble (Bessie).

Although the elements of war and politics are always so much a part of O'Casey's first three plays, it is the social evils of society that can be said to be his paramount concern. As John Gassner states: "Here in the slums, O'Casey seems to imply, is the real evil that men must conquer, and every other cause should be secondary to this problem."

O'Casey's interest in socialism can be traced to his background and his concern for his fellow human beings. At this point in his writing career, however, it has but minor importance in his dramas. His first two plays, The Shadow of a Gunman and Juno make no direct reference to socialism or Socialists. In The Plough and the Stars he does introduce a Socialist in the character of the Young Covey, but he makes him a somewhat weak and ineffectual character. Although some of his speeches have the ring of sincerity, the overall impression given by Young Covey is one of groping and immaturity. George Jean Nathan sums up his impression of the Young Covey in these words: "There is the young Irish liberal and dreamer, constantly mouthing an ill-assimilated amount of sociological information." O'Casey paints the Young Covey in extremely human terms and is never guilty of making him a paragon of virtue or intelligence. For instance, there is a bit of back-handed laughter on O'Casey's part at the young Covey in the following passage from the play:

> THE COVEY. Look here, comrade, there's no such thing as an Irishman, or an Englishman, or a German or a Turk; we're all only human bein's. Scientifically speakin', it's all a question of the accidental gatherin' together of molly-cewels an' atoms.
>
> FLUTHER. Mollycewels an' atoms! D'ye think I'm goin' to listen to you thryin' to juggle Fluther's mind with complicated conundhrums of mollycewels an' atoms?
>
> THE COVEY. There's nothin' complicated in it. There's no fear o' th' Church tellin' you that mollycewels is a stickin' together of millions of atoms o' sodium, carbon, potassium o' iodide, etcetera, that, accordin' to th' way they're mixed, make a flower, a fish, a star that you see shinin' in th' sky, or a man with a big brain like me, or a man with a little brain like you!
>
> FLUTHER. There's no necessity to be raisin' your voice; shoutin's no manifestin' forth of a growin' mind.

O'Casey has some good-natured fun at the expense of certain individuals who would call themselves Socialists. Corporal Stoddart, the Tommy, who appears in the last act to take away the body of little Mollser, becomes involved in a discussion with the Young Covey:

> CORPORAL STODDART. Was she plugged?
>
> THE COVEY. Ah, no; died o' consumption.
>
> CORPORAL STODDART. Ow, is that hall? Thought she moight 'ave been plugged.

THE COVEY. Is that all? Isn't it enough? D'ye know, comrade, that more die o' consumption than are killed in th' wars? An' it's all because of th' system we're livin' undher?

CORPORAL STODDART. Ow, I know. I'm a Sowcialist moiself, but I 'as to do my dooty.

THE COVEY. Dooty! Th' only dooty of a Socialist is th' emancipation of th' workers.

CORPORAL STODDART. Ow, a man's a man, an 'e 'as to foight for 'is country, 'asn't 'e?

FLUTHER. You're not fightin' for your country here, are you?

THE COVEY. Fight for your counthry! Did y'ever read, comrade, Jenersky's *Thesis on the Origin, Development, an' Consolidation of th' Evolutionary Idea of the Proletariat?*

CORPORAL STODDART. Ow, cheese it, Paddy, cheese it!

There is little in the text of the play to justify Gassner's assertion that O'Casey "reflects international European socialism." The final impression of the young Covey's remarks is one of ineffectuality and immaturity. The character of the Young Covey reflects no high ideals or sentiments. O'Casey has him loot with the rest of them and has him remark: "Th' selfishness of that one—she waited till she got all she could carry before she's come to tell any one!" And when Fluther is too slow-moving in starting out on the looting party, the Young Covey remarks irritatedly: "Come on, man, an' don't be wastin' time." O'Casey in these three plays is the delineator of society, not an advocate of any particular type of social reform.

Mention has been made of the riots that occurred during the

presentation of *The Plough and the Stars*. It was not only O'Casey's lack of hero-worship and lack of obeisance for the exaggerated and often insincere patriotism that was then the order of the day that infuriated the audience, but his feeling that war and bloodshed were highly undesirable even for as worthy a cause as Irish independence. In addition, we can gather from his autobiography that side by side with his pacifism was the conviction that in spite of the loud huzza ringing out on all sides about freedom, he felt that national freedom alone did not solve the basic social problems of the people. Therefore, it is a combination of these two beliefs that made O'Casey question whether the sacrifices made by individuals were commensurate with the gains obtained. His plays reveal that, by and large, he did not think so. His great pity goes out to the innocent victims of heroic acts. We feel sympathy for Juno, who is left behind, rather than for Johnny, who met his death at the hands of gunmen; we mourn for the mad Nora rather than for her husband, Jack Clitheroe; we feel the great tragedy of Minnie Powell's needless sacrifice and disgust for the "heroics" of Donal Davoren; we brush aside a tear shed over the fate of poor little Mollser, but we feel little over the deaths of Maguire of the I.R.A. in *The Shadow of a Gunman* and of Lieutenant Langon of the Irish Volunteers in *The Plough and the Stars*.

O'Casey, at times, questions whether even one life is worth sacrificing for the cause, or whether the resultant misery to a mother, for instance, does not make the cause, even the victory of the cause, seem hollow and horrible. For instance, Mrs. Tancred's son is killed by gunmen, and a neighbor says to her as they prepare to accompany the body to the grave: "It's a sad journey we're goin' on, but God's good, an' the Republicans won't be always down." The anguish-filled mother replies: "Ah, what good is that to me now? Whether they're up or down— it won't bring me darlin' boy from the grave."

We shall have occasion more than once in our study of O'Casey to refer to his pacifism. At this stage of O'Casey's dramatic career, however, we must agree with Gwynn, who states:

"The convictions that show through Sean O'Casey's plays are those of a pacifist; the savage inhumanity of revolutionary methods revolts him; while futile displays of old-fashioned pub-lic-house patriotism disgust."

O'Casey is an admirer and defender of women. Throughout his plays it is the women who emerge as the noble, brave and sturdy ones, not the men. In his first play, it is Minnie Powell, in his second it is Juno, and in his third it is Nora and even the virago, Bessie Burgess, that we remember with respect. O'Casey's first three plays have heroines but no heroes. In part, at least, we can trace O'Casey's ennobling portrayal of women to the great courage and strength of his mother. It was Susan who had to keep the family together, to fight constantly against the repeated onslaughts of poverty, disease and death. Yet through it all, O'Casey tells us, she was uncomplaining and cheerful. It is no accident that O'Casey dedicated The Plough and the Stars to her with the words: "To the gay laugh of my mother at the gate of the grave." The story of Juno is the story of his own mother, and of innumerable unsung heroines of the Dublin slums. O'Casey salutes the working-class women, the first acknowledgment of their greatness to be observed in Irish drama. The working girl (Minnie Powell), the proletarian

41

mother (Juno), and the laborer's wife (Nora) supplant queens and rich men's mistresses, middle-class ladies and milkmaids as literary heroines.

O'Casey's attitude toward the church, an extremely important factor in the political and social life of Ireland, is not clearly defined in his first three plays. His characters refer to the church on many occasions, but no clear-cut delineation of its role in Irish life emerges. We must wait until he writes *Within the Gates* for a full-length portrait of the church.

It must be emphasized, however, that O'Casey was a Protestant in a predominantly Catholic section of Ireland. Thus, he was a non-conformist. This had certain advantages and disadvantages. The disadvantages were that as an outsider looking in he could share in the prevailing religious activity of the community only as a bystander; further, it exposed him to certain of the prejudices to which a member of a minority group is usually subjected. The advantages, however, outweighed the disadvantages. The very fact that he was an outsider allowed him to view the religious scene with a greater perspective; further, his portrayal of the church and religion was not bound by conscious or unconscious religious heritages and practices. But such problems had little importance at this time, for O'Casey chose to introduce the church only as background material.

As has already been mentioned, O'Casey was a rare phenomenon in Irish letters: he had come out of the slums to write about the slums. His background of self-education and literary interests are reflected in Seumas and Donal in *The Shadow of a Gunman*. Here are two slum-dwellers who, by all odds, should never quote Shelley to each other, if we use conventional yardsticks to measure the capacities and interests of tenement people.

Yet, a new age was creeping up on Ireland, an age in which certain people from the slums were emerging from the shadows of ignorance into the sunstreams of cultural interests. O'Casey was one of these individuals. It was a shock to some who refused to believe that "slum-lice" could develop wings. This refusal to believe is exemplified, for instance, by a review in the *Bookman* (London) of *The Shadow of a Gunman* in which we find the following:

"I don't quite believe in Seumas; I don't believe that if he had shared the poet's room for a hundred years he would have quoted Shelley at him, even ironically, nor have been more than vaguely aware of Shelley's name."

How could a peddler, the above passage implies, be interested in, let alone quote, passages from Shelley? The poor quoting Shelley—impossible! Yet, O'Casey himself proved that it was not impossible. And he added a rose to the loaf by including in his play two poor devils who are sensitive enough to overcome the stultifying influences of poverty and take up a book of Shelley, for instance, with loving hands and an understanding heart. It was as if O'Casey were hurling a long overdue challenge to people with money and leisure. The fruits of centuries of culture, he seems to be saying, can be enjoyed not only by the leisure class but also by the poor and work-besotted. The rose as well as the loaf: the poor in pocket do not have to be poor in mind.

O'Casey's presentation of Dublin life is sincere and accurate and stands as a living picture of the Irish War years. Horace Horsnell, emphasizing O'Casey's fidelity to life and events, writes:

"In presenting these pictures of Dublin under the Terror, he

43

spares neither friend nor foe. His Irish patriots, windbags, and poltroons are drawn as dispassionately as his egregious Black and Tans. One feels, even as one's blood boils, that if challenged he could produce chapter and verse for every episode and almost every speech. His perspective is beautifully free from bias."

Ashley Dukes comments on O'Casey's sincerity: "A passionate sincerity in the study of everyday life gives distinction to the plays of Sean O'Casey." One critic states that "Mr. O'Casey is always on the side of the angels," and another that "the only prayer to be heard on our stage today" is that of Juno when she cries: "Sacred Heart o' Jesus, take away our hearts o' stone, and give us hearts o' flesh! Take away this murdherin' hate, an' give us Thine own eternal love!"

But instead of the prayer being answered, O'Casey tells us in his next play, *The Silver Tassie*, that both God and man have betrayed and have been betrayed.

three

THE WIDENING HORIZON

Two years elapsed between the presentation of O'Casey's last play of the "Irish War Period," *The Plough and the Stars,* and his highly controversial play *The Silver Tassie.* During these two years O'Casey lived in England with his bride, Eileen Reynolds. He had obtained fame and a certain amount of financial security. No longer was it necessary for him to acknowledge the praise of friends on the success of his plays while working as a janitor in a workingmen's hall. His knock at the door of literature had been heard and he had been admitted with great fanfare. He had succeeded in "creating things out of his own life ... to make pictures himself; ay, pictures, too, that would be worth hanging in the Hallway for other people to see." Some writers would have gone soft or continued writing plays on the same themes as those that had brought success. O'Casey did neither. In his next play he showed tremendous intensity and dealt with a much broader and more penetrating theme than in any of his previous plays.

The Silver Tassie is a play on World War I, and describes the privations, sufferings, brutalities, stupidities and hopeless inutility of war. It is a violent protest against organized legal murder;

it is a militant pacifist's indictment of a society that would sanction and defend that murder.

In many important respects it is a departure from his previous plays: no longer are all the scenes laid in Dublin; one is set in France, another in a hospital ward, and still another in a football clubhouse, leaving only the opening scene of the play in a working-class apartment house. Although the major characters of the play are Irish, half of the characters in the play are non-Irish. Many of his characters are of proletarian background, but their class composition is not strongly stressed; the depiction of slumlife is not an important aspect of the play. No strong or noble character stands out from the crowd; Irish national politics is ignored; the technique of the play, especially in the second act, is expressionistic rather than realistic. Thus O'Casey's break with the technique and content characteristic of his previous plays was only a partial breaking away.

This drama stands as a transitional play between those of his "Irish War Period" and *Within the Gates*, which followed *The Silver Tassie*. It is a transitional play not only in regard to those aspects of his previous plays which he modified or ignored, but also in regard to those elements which he heightened or introduced. For instance, the church and religion, which have played a fairly minor role until now, receive star billing; war, which has been background music, now becomes the leading motif; bitterness, a new element, takes its place beside pity; nameless characters (in the second act) emerge as important forces; and, finally, his subjective pacifism changes to militant objective pacifism.

In the opening act of the play we find Sylvester Heegan, a docker, and his friend, Simon Norton, a checker on the docks, being harangued by Susie Monican, a young woman filled with religion, on the need for the two men to embrace God. They are rescued by Mrs. Foran, a neighbor, who has fled into the apartment to escape from the beating her husband, Teddy, is bent on administering to her. Soon, Mrs. Heegan, Sylvester's wife, enters. She is extremely worried that her son, Harry Heegan, a soldier on leave, will not return on time to his boat which is leaving for France. In a burst of excitement, Harry enters with Jessie, his girl, and Barney Bagnal, his soldier friend. Harry's boot has won the game for the Avondale Football Club, and for the third straight year his name will be inscribed on the silver tassie. As Harry, Jessie and Barney celebrate the victory, Mrs. Heegan keeps reminding him that he must hurry to catch the boat, while Susie, who had previously tried to influence the headstrong Teddy when he was pursuing his wife with a "God is watching you, God is watching you," reminds the boys that "the men that go with the guns are going with God." Finally, the three soldiers, Harry, Barney and Teddy, are hustled off to the boat as Mrs. Heegan, with a deep sigh of satisfaction, says: "Thanks be to Christ that we're after managin' to get the three of them away safely!"

The second act opens in a "lacerated ruin of what was once a monastery." Signs of war devastation are all around, sharpened by the figure of the Virgin and a crucifix prominently facing a huge howitzer. In a rapid series of expressionistic scenes we are introduced to the weariness and heartache of the soldiers, the pompousness of war officials, the dead and the dying being carried to a nearby Red Cross Station, the horror and misery of battle and the degradation and despair of men in battle. One soldier asks, "Wy'r we 'ere, wy'r we 'ere,—that's wot I wants to

47

know" and is given the enlightening answer by the others, "We're here because we're here, because we're here, because we're here!" The Visitor, a pompous official, surveys the scene and remarks that the soldiers should not have any leisure because it gives them "too much time to think. Nervy. Time to brood, brood; bad. Sap. Sap. Sap." But the wounded on stretchers chant a different tune:

> "Carry on, carry on to the place of pain,
> Where the surgeon spreads his aid, aid, aid.
> And we show man's wonderful work, well done,
> To the image God hath made, made, made,
> And we show man's wonderful work, well done,
> To the image God hath made! ...
> Carry on—we've one bugled reason why—
> We've 'eard and answer'd the call, call, call.
> There's no more to be said, for when we are dead,
> We may understand it all, all, all.
> There's no more to be said, for when we are dead,
> We may understand it all."

At the corporal's request to "honour that in which we do put our trust," the soldiers kneeling down in front of the big gun chant to the glory of the gun which has found the ear of God, the artists who have created over the ages dreams to make men strong to kill, the children reared to be soldiers, the women who have given the fruit of their wombs to dark graves, the youth dying before they have reached manhood, the joys of paradise when the enemy is defeated. At constant intervals the words, "We believe in God and we believe in thee," accentuate the chant. The Staff-Wallah screams to the soldiers:

48

"All the batsmen, every cook, every bitch's son that hides a whiff of courage in his veins, shelter'd vigour in his body, that can run, or can walk, even crawl—dig him out, shove him on."

The soldiers answer his cry with, "To the guns!" as the curtain falls amid the firing of guns and the bursting of shells.

The third act takes place in a hospital ward, where Sylvester, Simon, Teddy and Harry are patients and Susie is a nurse. The first two men are not seriously wounded, but poor Harry Heegan has been hit in the spine and has lost the use of his legs, and Teddy is blind. Susie is no longer interested as much in religion as she is in Forby Maxwell, a surgeon. Mrs. Heegan and Mrs. Foran visit the ward, but Jessie, now that Harry is a cripple, is much more interested in healthier specimens of mankind and takes up with Barney Bagnal. Susie suggests that if Harry will go out "among the beeches and the pines, when the daffodils are hanging out their blossoms, ... [he will] deepen ... [his] chance in the courage and renewal of the country." Harry, bitter over his fate and Jessie's desertion, answers her:

"I'll say to the pine, 'Give me the grace and beauty of the beech'; I'll say to the beech, 'Give me the strength and stature of the pine.' In a net I'll catch butterflies in bunches; I'll twist and mangle them between my fingers, and fix them wriggling on to mercy's banner. I'll make my chair a Juggernaut, and wheel it over the neck and spine of every daffodil that looks at me, and strew them dead to manifest the mercy of God and the justice of man!"

The Sister asks Harry to "pray to God, for wonderful He is in His doing toward the children of men." But the child of man, the helpless cripple, can only moan: 'God of the miracles, give a poor devil a chance, give a poor devil a chance!'

The last act takes us to the scene of Harry's former glory—the Avondale Football Club. Jessie is in the arms of Barney, Susie is waltzing around the room with Dr. Maxwell, and Harry and Teddy are alone with their misery. Jessie feels the eyes of Harry following her wherever she goes, and she complains to Barney that he "is pulling all the enjoyment out of the night. It makes me shiver to feel him wheeling after us." The doctor insists that it is too exciting for Harry and that he should go home. Harry agrees to go if they will allow him to drink wine from the silver tassie. They bring it to him but he dashes it to the floor. Harry, the cripple, who wishes that he "had the strength to do the things he sees" and Teddy, the blind man, who wishes that he "could see the things he has strength to do" prepare to leave the healthy ones behind them. As they leave, Harry cries: "The Lord hath given and man hath taken away!" and Teddy answers, "Blessed be the name of the Lord!" The curtain descends as Susie sings:

> "Time to look sad when we know,
> So let us be merry again.
> He is gone, we remain, and so
> Let him wrap himself up in his woe
> For he is a life on the ebb
> We a full life on the flow."

The Silver Tassie was rejected by the Abbey Theatre in 1928. The rejection gave rise to a prolonged and bitter controversy between Yeats and O'Casey. Yeats based his rejection of the play on the fact that O'Casey had intruded into the play with his own personal opinions, that there was no dominating character, that O'Casey had not been in the war and was writing on something he knew nothing about and was not even interested in. O'Casey answered Yeats by condemning him for his impudence in asserting that he was not interested in the war, or that he could not write a play about the war because he had not been on the battlefield. He asked if Shakespeare was at Actium or Philippi or if George Bernard Shaw was in the boats with the French. He dismissed the fact that he had no dominating character in the play and insisted that *The Silver Tassie* was a greater work than the highly successful *The Plough and the Stars*.

O'Casey consequently broke off his connections with the theatre that had discovered him. The Abbey, on the other hand, bogged down after the war with a long list of undistinguished plays, lost the dramatist who had saved it in 1923 and since then had been its greatest drawing card. To this very day it is a debatable question whether the Abbey was too narrow or O'Casey was too broad. However, Sean O'Faolain throws considerable light on the question in the following remarks:

"...The Abbey wanted more Junos and more Paycocks. But O'Casey didn't give a curse about Juno as Juno or the Paycock as the Paycock. He had thrown them at the public conscience of Ireland with fury in his heart, as Jonathan Swift threw Gulliver, and Dublin laughed at the pair of them. The Abbey had underestimated the *saevo indignatio* of Sean O'Casey and when he followed his Gulliver with his Brobdingnagians and Houyhnhnms, it was simply not amused."

We have here, then, one of several cases in literary history in which a humorous criticism of society (*Juno and the Paycock*) is accepted, but a serious and biting criticism of society (*The Silver Tassie*) meets with opposition. Yet, however strong and

51

bitter the criticism, O'Casey vowed that he would not write to suit critics or government policy. His next several plays were just as serious and biting as *The Silver Tassie*.

In *The Silver Tassie*, at no time does O'Casey take sides on the rightness or wrongness of the opposing forces in the war. He does not deal with the relative merits or demerits of the Central Powers or the Allies. It is not that O'Casey is not interested in this phase of the war, but that the human wreckage resulting from war makes the moral position of both sides indefensible. Partisan politics has little significance when suffering and death come on the scene. In this respect, O'Casey follows the pattern of thought that we have noticed in his previous plays. The main difference is in his approach to the problem. In his previous plays he merely delineates; in *The Silver Tassie* he condemns the forces he delineates. This is not to say that O'Casey is didactic, but that the very vigor of his attack, couched in brilliant dramatic terms, can leave but one impression—condemnation of the social forces that bring on and defend war.

In the second act of the play, O'Casey uses expressionistic forms instead of realistic ones. The use of one expressionistic act in the middle of three realistic ones has caused many critics to shudder. A typical reaction is the one in which a reviewer calls the play a "hotch-potch...as wooly as anything that can be written by an Expressionist with a headache..." O'Casey, in his book, *The Flying Wasp*, violently condemns those critics who would set themselves up as literary dictators, categorically stating what may or may not be included in a play. However, we are not concerned here with the technical phases or critical reactions to expressionism per se, but with the far-reaching social implications inherent in his use of expressionism.

The first, third and fourth acts are realistic, but O'Casey turned to expressionism in the second act because he felt that symbols rather than individuals were necessary in order to carry out his intention of portraying the effect of war on society. He was concerned not with this or that individual but with the mass. O'Casey did not wish the full tragedy of war to be seen only as the physical incapacitation of a Harry Heegan or a Teddy Foran, but as the physical, spiritual and intellectual degradation of the mass itself. War had made men into machines, or, at least, had attempted to do so. Remember the Visitor's fear that if the men had leisure they might think and the machine-like answer the soldier received when he asked why he was at the front. The conflict was not between men and men, but between man and machines, between God and the howitzer. Modern war was turning the individual into the mass to be swallowed up en masse by the machine. The howitzer was too powerful; even God was consumed by it.

O'Casey did not abolish the individual; war had done that. The lack of a hero or heroine in The Silver Tassie disturbed W. B. Yeats considerably. He was evaluating O'Casey's play by accepted standards of dramatic construction, and from that point of view he was probably correct in finding fault with the play. However, the question O'Casey raises over and over again in The Flying Wasp is: who is to determine what is standard, right or wrong, dramatically correct?

If the center of the dramatic action is to be this or that individual in society, then we shall probably have to use certain dramatic forms, but if the dramatic action is to center around no particular individual but society as a whole, or, in other words, if society is to be the hero, then other dramatic forms may have to be used.

The political and social implications, for instance, arising out of this new concept of society are of tremendous importance. The whole structure of a society based, rightly or wrongly, on the individual, becomes threatened by the concept of a society based upon the mass in which no individual can rise above the mass. Toller, in his play, *Masse Mensch*, exploits this idea. O'Casey, in *The Silver Tassie*, straddled the question by using both individuals and symbols. G. B. Shaw appreciated the problem that writers such as Toller and O'Casey were willing to deal with and wrote:

"There is a new drama rising from unplumbed depths to sweep the nice little bourgeois efforts of myself and my contemporaries into the dust bin; and your name will live as the man who didn't run away."

O'Casey didn't run away. Instead, he plunged even deeper into the problem, as an examination of *Within the Gates* will reveal.

four

PHANTASMAGORIA OF SOCIETY

In *Within the Gates* (1933) O'Casey breaks completely with Irish settings and characters. The action takes place in England in a public park, presumably Hyde Park. The characters are an unusual combination of individuals and symbols: individuals in that they have the flesh and blood reactions of human beings; symbols in that they represent defined segments of society.

Within the Gates has been called "an allegory of the modern world," "a dramatic poem," "a charade," "a humanitarian fantasy," "a panoramic play," "a twentieth-century morality play," "a symphony in cyclic style," and one critic, James Agate, dismisses it as "pretentious rubbish." One critic claims that it has "vacuity of content," another claims that it is "based on a new and integral faith in life," and still another claims that it "exposes the cheap shoddiness of modern society." The critics vary widely in their evaluation of the play. One critic sees the play as "a monument of dramatic art"; another as "a symbol of the confusion at once moral and esthetic which permeates so much of modern writing"; still another as "a drama that sweeps along through the loves and terrors of mankind ... Nothing so grand has arisen in our impoverished theatre since this reporter first

55

began writing of plays"; still another claims that he "doesn't know what Mr. O'Casey is driving at." One illustrious reviewer in *Theatre Arts Monthly* states that *Within the Gates* "is a work no actor can handle and no critic can praise with real conviction"; but in the same magazine eight months later we read that when produced "it comes out as a moving drama, with simple austerity, swinging merriment, beauty in music of word and color of scene and...tragedy too deep for tears."

Within the Gates is a difficult play to view dispassionately. The above welter of viewpoints is a testament of this fact. The play strikes hard and deep at many social institutions and moral precepts of present-day life. It has the power to offend or defend, depending upon one's point of view. The play contains optimism and pessimism, beauty and ugliness, comedy and tragedy. It both lifts to the heavens and crashes down to earth man's ideas about himself, his fellow man, and society at large. It is, indeed, one of the few plays in modern drama that has taken all of life for its theme. Because of this and because it lacks a definite plot, a detailed description of the play's action must be presented.

The gates of the park open—it is spring—the chorus of young boys and girls, representing trees and flowers, sings a song in praise of "our mother, the earth" for giving them the birds and blossoms again. The Bishop, who wants to get into closer contact with the people, and his sister, who looks with dismay at this idea, pass before us. Two tired Chair Attendants, each with a stiff leg, discuss bad legs, poverty and prayers, and walk out. The Dreamer, a young man, and the Atheist, a wiry man of fifty, appear. The Atheist tells of a young girl he has adopted, but who has now left him and has become a prostitute. The

Bishop, the Two Attendants, and a Policewoman rhapsodize about the glories of nature and God. The Atheist challenges their statements. The Young Man in Plus-Fours follows the Scarlet Lady across the stage. The Policewoman follows this charming couple. Two Nursemaids wheeling perambulators stroll on the stage, exchange a little gossip, and leave, followed by the glances of the Gardener. The Two Attendants reappear and make believe they are not affected by the sounds of the sombre music of the Down-and-Outs. The Gardener, talking to the Dreamer, gives us a hint of his intentions with the Young Whore. The Dreamer, inspired by spring, reclines on the grass to write a poem. The Gardener sings a song about "dancing with a girl in a hall at the end of the day." Young couples walk on the stage and join in the song. The Young Whore enters anxiously, looks around, and goes off. Two Evangelists move their lips, but are not heard above the singing. The Atheist tells the Young Whore he will not be her guardian any longer. The Atheist leaves and the Salvation Army Officer, who has overheard the conversation, rhapsodizes about God while massaging the Young Whore's knee. He leaves for his meeting, and the Gardener comes in. The Young Whore demands to know if he will marry her. He hedges about, but when she insists on a definite answer, he says he will not marry her. The young Whore goes out, followed by the Man in Plus-Fours. The Foreman bawls out the Gardener for speaking to women while on the job. The first scene ends with the Young Whore in the hands of the Policewoman, charged with enticing the Young Man in Plus-Fours.

The gates open for the second scene—it is summer—the chorus, in song, urges the people to leave their stuffy offices and enjoy the glories of nature. The Two Nursemaids, with their perambulators, are approached by the Bishop, who still wishes to come into contact with the masses. The two Nursemaids leave, giggling at the pomposity of the Bishop. He next approaches the Two Attendants, who have been dismissed because of being too old, and strikes up a conversation with them. The Two Attendants ask him for a pound or two to reinforce his religious sincerity. He refuses and they are no longer interested in God. Again, the Attendants hear the mournful sounds of the Down-and-Outs. The Young Whore appeals to the Bishop for aid. He refuses to help a prostitute. The Young Whore's mother appears and begins to beat the girl. The Bishop intervenes. The Old Woman, upon hearing the Bishop's voice, intimates that he is the man who seduced her in her youth. The Bishop is frightened and tries to stop the Old Woman from beating the Young Whore, realizing she is his daughter. It is the Dreamer who stops the beating. The Bishop leaves, giving the Dreamer two pounds to give to the Young Whore. As the Dreamer serenades the Young Whore with a song and a pound note, the Gardener, the Bishop and the Young Man in Plus-Fours come on stage. The second scene closes with the Young Whore going off with the Young Man in Plus-Fours as the music, growing louder, mocks the three men.

The gates of the park open—it is autumn—the Two Attendants, in the semifinal stage of decay, are half-asleep on a bench. The Young Man in Plus-Fours is leading the community singing which extols the glory of the earth. He leaves, when the singing is over, to follow the Scarlet Woman. The Two Attendants are awakened and begin to talk about the gold standard. The Two Nursemaids, accompanied by a little boy, stroll on the stage and then leave. Several men march onto the stage and begin to read their newspapers, upon which are printed in bold type Murder, Rape, Divorce, Racing, Suicide, Execution and Great Cricketer Talks About God. The Bishop is seen in the shadows. The Young Whore enters, a little tipsy, and heckles the men who are "sucking in holy thoughts of holy wisdom" from their newspapers. The Young Whore defies the death she feels approaching, and shouts that she'll "die dancing"; the readers demand that they be allowed to read in peace; the Bishop, who has aged considerably, begs the Young Whore to stop her ranting. All he gets for his trouble is violent abuse from her. "The Readers fold up their papers...and go out as they came in, to staccato notes plucked from a fiddle string." Tht Two Attendants return. The Young Whore, exhausted from her raving, is approached by the Bishop who tries to calm her with impromptu sermons about God. She demands to know why he is following her. He brushes aside her question and offers to place her in a convent. She mocks him for this and in a wild display of devil-may-care flings two of her last three bills to the wretched Attendants.

From the distance is heard the drum-tap and chant of the Down-and-Outs. With the exception of the Bishop, all are frightened by the sound. The black silhouettes of the Down-and-Outs pass by. "They are bent, tattered and hopeless wrecks of old and young men and women; they go by in a slow and miserable manner, chanting their miserere to the monotonous tap, tap, tap of the drum-beat." The chant itself is about a dead hope and a dead faith.

The Bishop urges Two Placarded Evangelists and the Two Attendants to join "the poor, the sacred Aristocracy of God!"

The Two Evangelists angrily retort that they are "in the 'ands of Gord already!" and the Two Attendants refuse to believe that the Down-and-Outs are looking for them. The Bishop warns the Young Whore that the Down-and-Outs came very close to her and urges her to seek God. She refuses, but less decisively than before. The Atheist, the Foreman and the Man with the Stick enter and excitedly and confusedly argue about God. A Young Salvation Army Officer enters the argument. The discussion is ended abruptly by the excited entrance of the Young Whore, who asks for a song because her heart is ready to stop beating. She throws her arms about the Young Salvation Army Officer's neck. He spurns her with a word about God and mounts on a platform to speak about salvation for sinners. The Salvationists join in a chorus. The Young Whore and the Two Attendants kneel before the platform. The Dreamer enters and urges the Young Whore to go with him. She is torn between the promised joy with the Dreamer and the promised land of the Salvationists. The gates close as she goes off with the Dreamer while the Salvationists pray for her soul.

The gates open for the fourth and last scene—it is winter. There are two platforms on the stage. On the one is a sign, "There Must Be A God," on the other is, "There Can't Be A God." The Bishop is seen looking for the Young Whore. The Man with the Stick enters and heckles the speaker behind the "There Must Be A God" platform. The Bishop's Sister runs on and off the stage calling for Gilbert, the Bishop. The Two Platform Speakers argue. The Man in the Trilby, the Man in the Bowler Hat and the Man with the Stick argue about space and time, and exit. The Bishop shakes off his sister, who tries to make him go home, and continues his frantic searching. The

Young Man in Plus-Fours stops before the platforms. An audience! The speakers shout their message, but the Scarlet Woman is the victor as the Young Man in Plus-Fours follows her off the stage. The Old Woman enters and tonelessly mourns that "the golden life of England has gone into the bellies of the worms." The Speakers, unable to get an audience, fold their platforms and leave.

The Two Nursemaids, the Guardsman and the Young Man enter. The two men gossip about their superiors, as the girls interrupt constantly with "Gi's another squeeze." The couples leave as the Old Woman enters. She places a wreath at the base of a statue of a dragoon, and sings a song about youth that is dead. As she goes out, she bitterly urges in a song, "May God in a rage smite the world to its end."

The former trio of disputants enter, arguing about the unconscious. They are joined by the Man in the Burberry, who incoherently shouts about the world being upside down. After his insane ravings, the neurotic Man in the Burberry slinks away and the disputants disperse. The Young Whore, leaning on the Dreamer's arm, begs him to find the Bishop. The Dreamer unsuccessfully urges her to get comfort from him. He leaves to find the Bishop. The Young Man in Plus-Fours approaches and strokes the girl's knee. She takes no notice of him and he goes out. The Gardener, who had jilted her, approaches and asks for a kind word for old times' sake. She ignores him and he leaves, lilting to himself about "dancing with a girl in a hall at the end of the day."

The Old Woman enters, looking for the Bishop, followed by the Bishop's Sister, who is on the same errand. Upon seeing the Young Whore, she gives the girl a merciless tongue lashing.

61

The Two Evangelists and the Two Attendants, their legs tottering, enter. In the distance is heard the drum-tap and chant of the Down-and-Outs. The girl rushes over to the Bishop, who has appeared on the stage, and asks for his blessing. The Bishop tries, but cannot bring himself to bless her. The Dreamer appears. The Bishop's Sister curses the Young Whore. The chant of the Down-and-Outs is heard in their death-song. The Young Whore cries that they have come for her at last. The Two Chair Attendants beg God to spare them, because they are no worse than other men. The Two Evangelists pray to God to spare them, because they have always honored pain and sighing in the name of God. The Down-and-Outs are very near. The Young Whore again begs the Bishop to bless her. He replies with definiteness that she will find safety and penance only with the Down-and-Outs. She approaches them, but is stopped by the Dreamer. He urges her not to give in but to die with a song. They dance. The Young Whore becomes frightened; the Dreamer urges her on to dance; the Down-and-Outs come closer; the Young Whore collapses; she asks the Bishop to help her hand make the sign of the cross; he does. The Down-and-Outs envelop in their ranks the Two Evangelists, the Old Woman and the Two Chair Attendants. They exit with the voice of the Old Woman calling appealingly from among them the name of the Bishop. The Dreamer bids a final farewell to his dying sweetheart.

The gates close with the Bishop uttering in low and grief-stricken tones: "She died making the sign of the cross, she died making the sign of the cross!"

In order to round out the picture that O'Casey presents in the play, it is necessary to understand the symbols that he uses.

Definitiveness in a play such as we have outlined, is not completely possible.

One critic's complaint that the play is an example of moral and esthetic confusion has a certain validity. It is the confusion of modern life, however, not the confusion of O'Casey that the play presents. To expect order in an orderless world, to expect a playwright to wave his magic wand of genius and bring order out of chaos is to expect the impossible. O'Casey has given us a picture of life, and if that picture shows intellectual, moral and social confusion, the fault lies not with the writer but with society.

O'Casey, in an article written just before the opening of the play in New York, has given us what he feels to be the meaning of the symbols he used. Commenting on O'Casey's explanation of the symbols, Gassner states that "the author's own explanations of his allegory are abstruse and the precise meaning of his symbolism is open to discussion." Even though there is some justification for this remark, we must repeat that preciseness and absolute clarity are difficult, if not impossible, to achieve in a play that is based upon the confusion of modern life. The following is O'Casey's explanation:

"The Dreamer, symbol of a noble restlessness and discontent; of the stir in life that brings to birth new things and greater things than those that were before; of the power realizing that the urge of life is above the level of conventional morality; of ruthlessness to get near to the things that matter, and sanctify them with intelligence, energy, gracefulness and song; of rebellion against stupidity; and of the rising intelligence in man that will no longer stand, nor venerate, nor shelter those whom poverty of spirit has emptied of all that is worth while in life.

63

"*The Atheist,* symbol of those who, trying to get rid of God, plant Him more firmly on His throne.

"*The Young Whore,* symbol of those young women full of life and a fine energy, gracious and kind, to whom life fails to respond, and who are determined to be wicked rather than virtuous out of conformity or fear.

"*The Chair Attendants,* symbols of life's wreckage who, with the Evangelists, are wasting life by living it.

"*The Evangelists,* symbol of those preachers who daub the glories of God with mockeries.

"*The Scarlet Woman,* symbol of those young women who think their legs are the pillars of the world and of wisdom, who giving, give not, and who live far away from life.

"*The Young Man in Plus-Fours,* symbol of those young and old men whose whole life is an interest in the surface of women.

"*The Gardener,* symbol of the multitude mind moving on head down, shrinking from thought, and finding inspiration in all things cheap and everything easy. Seeking the things that present no risk and leave no risk behind them.

"*The Old Woman,* symbol of those who stand still, think the little world round was born to serve them, and that when they die, life dies too.

"*The Policewoman,* symbol of woman dressed in a little brief authority.

"*The Young Salvation Army Officer,* symbol of the colored sob-stuff in organized religion that reflects no gleam from the mind of God, and brings no gleam to the mind of man.

"*The Disputants,* symbols of those who hear and give great arguments, but are none the wiser for it all.

"*Nursemaids* and *Guardsmen,* symbols of those simple souls who take life as they find it, and, without much effort, make the best of it.

"*The Choruses*, symbol of the energy and stir of life.

"*Down-and-Outs*, symbols of all who are dead to courage, fortitude, and the will to power; of those to whom a new thought or a new idea brings terror and dismay; of those who turn the struggle of life into a whine; of those, young or old, rich or poor, who in thought, word, and deed, give nothing to life, and so are outcasts from life even as they live; even so."

With the use of these symbols, O'Casey, through action and dialogue, has projected on the stage his picture of modern society. The picture that we get is of a society that has exchanged ennobling human values for gross material ones. The song of the chorus in the first scene, in which the coming of spring is heralded, may be taken as the promise of beauty and joy that life can hold in store for mankind. The final chorus of the Down-and-Outs in the last scene, in which it is winter and we hear a sigh instead of a song, may well mean the betrayal of that promise. The fate of man, however, is not only with the Down-and-Outs, but can be, if man is willing to travel the road, with the Dreamer. Thus, the total impression we may receive from the play is one in which life is depicted, according to one viewpoint, "against a background of eternal things, symbolized by shadowy processions on the way to nothingness," or, according to another point of view, "an escape into a golden dream-life of eternal freedom."

O'Casey has devoted much of his play to the place of religion and the church in modern life. The Bishop's fumbling attempt to get close to the common people is an admission that the church has strayed away from them. The Bishop remarks: "The

Church must keep alive, alive o, and up-to-date . . . Get amongst the people; get them to talk with us, joke with us, then we may expect them to pray with us." This suggests that it has lost touch with the people. A reason for this may be found in the Bishop's Sister's comment on this aspiration: "This idea of getting in touch with common people is stupid, dear. They'll simply grill you with mockery. Once lose your dignity and you're done."

O'Casey feels that the church has become a place of gloom and no longer sheds the light of hope and joy. The Dreamer underscores this idea when he bitterly remarks: "They cancel life with their livid love of God!" He feels that the church has been too eager to welcome the good, solid, respectable citizen into its fold instead of the less refined, less stable, less socially illustrious member of society. In one of the most dramatic speeches in the play, the Young Whore emphasizes this point. The Bishop has threatened to call the police if she does not leave him alone, and she replies:

"Easy way of getting over a difficulty by handing it over to a policeman. Get back, get back, please; gangway, gangway, there. Policemen making a gangway for Jesus Christ. You and your goodness are no use to God. If Christ came again, He'd have to call, not the sinners, but the righteous to repentance. Go out into the sun and pick the yellow primroses! Take your elegant and perfum'd soul out of the stress, and stain, the horrid cries, the noisy laugh of life, an' go out into the sun, an' pick the yellow primroses! When you go to where your God is throned, tell the gaping saints you never soiled a hand in Jesu's service. Tell them a pretty little whore, well on her way to hell, once tempted you to help her; but you saved yourself by the calm and cunning of a holy mind, an' went out into the sun to pick the yellow primroses, leaving her, sin-soddened, in the strain, the stain, the horrid cries, an' the noisy laugh of life. Tell them you were ever calm before the agony in other faces, an', an' the tip of your finger never touched a brow beaded with a bloody sweat! A tired Christ would be afraid to lean on your arm. Your Christ wears a bowler hat, carries a cane, twiddles his lavender gloves, an' sends out gilt-edged cards of thanks to callers. Out with you, you old shivering sham, an' go away into the sun to pick the yellow primroses!"

O'Casey does not attack God or religion, as such, but insists that organized religion embodied in the church has lost its way. He himself sums up his attitude toward it in this manner:

"It [the play] shows organized religion, good-natured and well-intentioned, unable to find a word or invent an action that will give to life the help it needs. It's life half running out to meet life and the other half running away again."

The yellow press is exposed not only as a cheapening influence, but also as a reflection of the interests and ideals of a society that has become degenerate and decadent. The order of the day is murder, rape, divorce, racing, suicide, execution—the headlines that appear on the newspapers that the stolid middle-class gentlemen read. The Young Whore comments:

"Oh Lucifer, Lucifer, who has caused all newspapers, stars of the morning and stars of the evening, to be written for our learning, grant that we may so read that we may always find punch in them, hot stuff in them, and sound tips in them, so that both outwardly in our bodies, and inwardly in our souls, we get closer and closer to Thee!"

O'Casey has included in his play a picture of many sections

67

of society and has described the weaknesses of each of them. The bourgeoisie, in the characters of The Man in the Bowler Hat, The Man with the Stick and The Man in the Trilby Hat, are smug and misinformed; the "service" segment of the working-class, in the characters of the Gardener, the Nursemaids and the Two Attendants (when they are employed), is pictured as riddled through with cheapening thoughts, middle-class propriety and brassy patriotism; the outcasts from life, the Down-and-Outs, are a drag and a drug upon the body of society; the financially comfortable and socially elect, in the character of the Bishop's Sister, are narrow-minded, selfish and incapable of feeling the suffering of those who are less fortunate than themselves.

In the very depiction of the lack of faith that exists in the modern world, *Within the Gates* emerges as a powerful cry for a revived and vigorous faith in man and life.

five

JOHN BULL AND THE OTHER ISLAND

By 1940, O'Casey had lived for more than a dozen years in England. During this time he had ample time to compare English national characteristics with those of his own Irish folk. He reflected on the differences between these two people, so close together geographically, yet so far apart in temperament and historical development.

He came to the conclusion that a play on the two countries was an ideal subject, not for a heavy tragic play, but for a light farcical one in which the presentation of the differences between the two peoples would allow for an enjoyable and enlightening evening in the theatre. G. B. Shaw had been intrigued with the same idea and *John Bull's Other Island* had been the result. The theme was of sufficient dramatic stature to be used by another Irishman. There would be no shame attached to using the same idea; he had never made a secret of his admiration for Shaw. As far back as 1915 or so, he had thought of him as the cleverest Irishman of them all, a man who had helped Ireland by making her own people understand her, a man whose play about the Irish and the British he had started at tea time and had not put down until the break of day. He would write down his views on John Bull and the other island: *Purple Dust* (1940) was the result.

Although the play has been hailed as a brilliant comedy, a play which one critic states is "...an enormously amusing comedy which spoofs the more obvious English types and contrasts them with Irish wit and wiliness," and which George Jean Nathan calls "...a completely original, richly imaginative and beautifully written fanciful farce-comedy so full of reputable laughter that one would think it should find a producer overnight, even a producer among our peculiar lot," the play has had few professional productions. It was published in 1940 when the British were courageously fending off the Nazi invaders, and there were few producers who were willing to satirize the English at such a time. In this connection, Richard Watts, Jr., the American critic, remarks:

"*Purple Dust* is a superb comedy in both its beauty and its rowdiness, but had it been produced here, when planned, at the time of the blitz in England, its waspish stings at the expense of certain British pretensions might have aroused political resentment that would have handicapped its great merit."

The above comment does seem to be true not only for the United States but also for England. For instance, James Agate, the English critic, his anger aroused at what he considers O'Casey's lack of respect and support for the British people at a time when they were fighting for their very existence, calls the play "...a witless lampoon at the expense of the English too busy fighting for freedom to answer back."

The play is set in an Irish rural district. Two wealthy Englishmen, Basil Stoke and Cyril Poges, have acquired an old Tudor-Elizabethan mansion in which they have installed themselves and their Irish mistresses, Souhaun and Avril. They are determined to repair the ramshackle mansion, to create therein the grace of a vanished day and live the lives of rural gentlemen. Three Irish workmen and their foreman, O'Killigain, are given the task of making the house livable.

It is not long, however, before the Englishmen discover that it is a difficult task to re-create the past and to transplant themselves from the comforts of London to the relative primitiveness of the Irish countryside. Unable to forget their English customs, unwilling to give up their interests in business which constantly remind them of England, and incapable of understanding the Irish who plague them on all sides, they find that life becomes one difficult situation after another. Irish temperament clashes with English temperament, working-class outlooks conflict with bourgeois outlooks, rural mannerisms collide with city mannerisms until the entire household is in an uproar. The rains come and the flood-waters rise. The Irish girls, tired of their old stuffy Englishmen and entranced by the music and romance of the Irish, run off with two workers.

The Englishmen, determined to see it through, disregard warnings that they should leave in order to escape the flood. The play ends with the waters engulfing the house and the Englishmen. Poges moans: "My comfort's gone, and my house of pride is straining towards a fall. Would to God I were in England, now that winter's here!"

Although the spirit and action of the play is one of broad comedy, O'Casey slyly injects into the farce trenchant observations on the English and Irish. However, his selection of types, the class position of the English and the Irish characters, and the various situations in which he places them, give the Gaels

71

a distinct nod of approval over their visitors from across the Irish Sea.

The Englishmen are pictured as two fools; the Irish as saturated with the type of common sense native to people close to the earth; the Englishmen are from the bourgeoisie and display all the worst characteristics and few of the best characteristics of that class; the Irishmen are from the working-class and show all the best features and few of the worst features of their class; the Englishmen, away from their native land, in a country which they neither have the ability nor the desire to understand, are uncomfortable; the Irishmen are perfectly at ease in the land of their birth and upbringing. Yet, even though the contest of Irish vs. English has been set up in a somewhat unfair way, the two-hour brawl is interesting and enlightening.

The history of Ireland, in many respects, has been the history of English domination. The play takes place after most of Ireland had obtained its freedom. Yet the old hatreds remain and the underdog's desire to see his former master grovelling in the dust is still strong. A workman emphasizes this feeling when he says:

"Our poets of old have said it often: time'll see the Irish again with wine an' ale on th' table before them; an' th' English, barefoot, beggin' a crust in a lonely sthreet, an' th' weather frosty."

The fierce pride of the men of Erin for their great cultural traditions, as well as their marked characteristic of never allowing anyone to forget them, is underscored in the speech of one of the workers after Cyril Poges, with English superiority, has called him a fool:

"Comin' over here, thinkin' that all the glory an' grandeur of

72

the world, an' all the might of man, was stuffed into a bulgin' purse, an' stickin' their tongue out at a race that's oldher than themselves by a little like a thousand years, greater in their beginnin' than they are in their prime; with us speakin' with ayse the mighty languages o' the world when they could barely gurgle a few sounds, sayin' the rest in the movement of their fingers.... Hammerin' out handsome golden ornaments for flowin' cloak an' tidy tunic we were, while you were busy gatherin' dhried grass, an' dyin' it blue, to hide the consternation of your middle parts; decoratin' eminent books with glowin' colour an' audacious beauty were we, as O'Killigain himself will tell you, when you were still a hundhred score o' years away from even hearin' of the alphabet."

The English, as we can imagine, do not share the above exalted opinion of Ireland and the Irish. Poges replies to the above sentiments with, "there's Erin, the tear and the smile in her eye for you!" Basil, after being thrown by an Irish horse, cries: "Irresponsible, irresponsible, like the people!" It is Poges, however, who passes the often heard, the historic opinion of Englishmen about Ireland when he remarks: "Oh, what a terrible country to have anything to do with! ... what an awful country to be living in! A no-man's land; a waste land; a wilderness!"

The Irish, as we can imagine also, do not have any higher regard for the English than their cousins from across the sea have for them. O'Killigain views the British as "rascals, thieves and big-pulsed hypocrites," and predicts that "in a generation or so the English Empire will be remembered only as a half-forgotten nursery rhyme!"

Imperialism, in modern times, when the ideal of national

73

determination has become accepted even by imperial-minded Britain itself, is not easy to defend. Poges, however, always hearkening back to the past, expresses the viewpoint of the die-hard Englishman in the following passage:

"All the Irish are the same. Bit backward perhaps, like all primitive peoples, especially now, for they're missing the example and influence of the gentry; but delightful people all the same. They need control, though; oh yes, they need it badly."

It is the same Poges, nevertheless, who, while making this sort of statement out of one corner of his mouth, can, from the other corner, hurl a burning indictment against the clergy:

"Oh, these priests, these priests! Thick as weeds in this poor country. Opposed to every decent thought that happens not to have come from them. Sealing with seven seals any book an intelligent human being would wish to read. Ever on guard to keep the people from growing out of infancy."

In apparent sincerity, O'Casey has Poges say: "We, sir, are a liberty-loving people, and have always striven to preserve perfect—perfect, mind you—freedom of thought, not only in our own land, but throughout the whole world." When the same Poges a moment later, however, utters phrases that every nationalist in every country has uttered at one time or another, we begin to realize that O'Casey was merely leading the English on to a high peak of virtue so that he could throw them all the harder into the abyss below. Poges bombastically announces:

"But every right-minded man the world over knows, or ought to know, that wherever we have gone, progress, civilisation, truth, justice, honour, humanity, righteousness, and peace have followed at our heels. In the Press, in the Parliament, in the pulpit, or on the battlefield, no lie has ever been uttered by us, no false claim made, no right of man infringed, no law of God ignored, no human law, national or international, broken."

O'Casey reveals to us the various mannerisms and traditions of the English that have been described by many writers—the importance of family background, loyalty to the king, steadiness, efficiency, order. Poges probably reflects O'Casey's view of the English when he says:

"I believe in efficiency! I demand efficiency from myself, from everyone. Do the thing thoroughly and do it well: that's English. The word given, and the word kept: That's English. And I'm an Englishman!"

Ireland and the Irish fare much better at O'Casey's hands. There is little in the play that is critical of them, except, perhaps, their unbridled passion for the past, which makes them lose sight of the present. O'Casey has put them close to the rail; they just couldn't lose. As one reviewer commented: "It is the inequality and unreality of the contest which has driven Mr. O'Casey to flick it up with knock-about."

By the time O'Casey wrote *Purple Dust* in 1940 it was necessary to "flick it up with knock-about." Many of the burning issues that had plagued Irish-English relations for hundreds of years had been settled. In his next plays, however, he deals with political and social issues that are far from settled, issues which are dividing the world into two opposing camps, each with its own ideology and methodology. We may be sure that these plays contain little "knock-about," but rather these plays "set 'em up, knock 'em down and drag 'em out."

six

THE RED HORIZON

The political aspects of life have always played an important role in the plays of O'Casey, but in *The Star Turns Red* (1940) politics, with its economic, social, religious and personal ramifications, is portrayed. The dynamic issues of communism, fascism, trade unionism, the role of the state and religion in politics, and the individual as a political being are presented in sharp, decisive terms. The struggle for political power between the Right and the Left is the underlying theme; the delineation of the forces that make up and influence these two opposing camps forms the dramatic structure of the play.

O'Casey's world in *The Star Turns Red* is a world of opposites in which the middle way has ceased to exist. All members of society must choose sides, social and religious bodies must align themselves with one of the two opposites, no compromise is possible, the fight for political supremacy between the proletariat and the bourgeoisie can end only in a complete victory for one of the two camps. O'Casey sees the proletariat emerging as the victor.

The pacifism that we observed in *The Silver Tassie* has disappeared; the contention that even one life lost may be too high a price to pay in order to gain a political objective, brought out so vividly in the cases of Minnie, Nora and Harry Heegan, is supplanted by the thesis that struggle must bring on sacrifice, sacrifice may result in death and the death of one or a thousand and one is a necessary, though undesirable, step toward the realization of political goals.

It is not possible to know exactly why O'Casey chose this highly political theme for a play. However, by fitting together certain facts from his life with certain events from recent history, it is possible to find certain reasons for his choice of theme. O'Casey's deep interest in socialism, his activities in various working-class organizations, his secretaryship of a workers' military organization, the Citizen Army, the years of toil and poverty he experienced as an unskilled laborer have been noted as well as his great interest in the social problems of the people of the Dublin slums, victims of war and outcasts of society. His deep sympathy for the poor has been apparent throughout his plays. In addition to these factors, however, it may be assumed from various references that he makes in the play now under discussion, that the political events of the 1930's affected him deeply. In the play he has several passages on the civil war in Spain; the Nazi seizure of power in Germany is mirrored in the characters, organizations and events of the drama; alignment of the Catholic church with the Franco forces finds its parallel in the alignment of the Catholic church with the Saffron Shirts in The Star Turns Red. These events had a marked influence on his outlook, pushed him further and further to the Left, impelled him to present his views on many of the burning issues of the day at the same time that he was presenting the larger, over-all picture of the political and ideological struggle that is rocking the very foundations of society.

The play is dedicated "to the men and women who fought through the great Dublin lockout in nineteen hundred and thirteen" and takes place "tomorrow, or the next day." In the first act, we are introduced to the home of the Old Man and the Old Woman, which is being torn asunder by the violent hatred that their two sons, Jack, a Communist, and Kian, a Fascist, have for each other. The old folks must take sides: we find the Old Man has a tendency to agree with Kian, while the Old Woman sympathizes more with Jack. Julia, the daughter of a neighbor, Michael, is also a Communist and the sweetheart of Jack. Although as staunch a Communist as Jack, she urges him not to attend a strikers' demonstration but to go to a dance with her. He refuses and leaves the house, with Julia bitterly complaining: "Asking me to give up everything! I'm as good a Communist as he is; better, for where I'm working it's harder for a girl than a man to be one." Joybell, "a Catholic flag-waver," enters, and Julia teasingly parades in front of him to see whether he is as unconscious of a woman as he pretends. Unable to resist her baiting of him, he suddenly crushes her to him. Julia flings him away from her and Joybell dashes out. The Lord Mayor enters and invites the Old Man to help in the Christmas celebration. In the course of the conversation, he reveals himself as a supporter of the Saffron Shirts, a Fascist organization. He urges the Old Man to use his influence to bring Jack to his senses and have him leave the ranks of the Communists.

The Red Priest, a supporter of the Saffron Shirts and a violent opponent of the Communists and the strikers, and the Brown

Priest, a man close to the people, enter, a little before Jack returns. They are followed, in a few moments, by Kian and several members of the Saffron Shirts, who have come to warn Jack to give up his activities. The Red Priest supports the Saffron Shirts in their request. Julia, in an attempt to shield Jack, slaps the Leader across his face, and she is ordered to be taken away and whipped in order to teach her good manners. The Brown Priest tries to intervene in her behalf, but the Red Priest silences him. "I ask you to keep silence, and I order you to obey. To a priest, the first step to heaven is obedience, the second step is obedience, and the third step is obedience. Let what is to do be done." As she is led away, Jack says: "This shall be remembered unto you, dead-hearted priest, when the hour strikes for the workers to will the way to power!"

Michael, Julia's father, who has heard what has happened to his daughter, enters and protests violently. He attempts to strike the Leader, but before he can do so Kian shoots him. He dies, murmuring to Jack: "Now, my fist—close it. Now, my arm—raise it, lift it high. Lift it up, lift it up in the face of these murdering bastards—the Clenched Fist!"

The second act takes place in the headquarters of the General Workers' Union. Brallain, Eglish, Caheer and the Secretary, all union leaders, and the Red Priest are discussing Red Jim, the leader of the strikers.

The union leaders are pictured as men who have become unconcerned with the problems of the workers now that they have soft union jobs. Red Jim, patterned after Jim Larkin, the head of the 1913 strike, is pictured as strong, determined in speech and action, and a great leader of men.

The union leaders and the Red Priest agree that Red Jim

must be silenced. Brannigan, a right-hand man of Red Jim's, enters and demands his insurance money. The striking difference between Brannigan's militancy and the union leaders' timidity is portrayed. Sheasker, another union leader, enters, and shortly thereafter the Brown Priest. The Brown Priest, concerned over the safety of Red Jim, warns the union leaders that Red Jim's life is in danger. Red Jim appears, thanks the Brown Priest for his concern, admonishes Brannigan for being drunk, censures the union officials for their betrayal of the strikers, and, after placing Brannigan in charge of the office, leaves. The act ends with Brannigan, flanked by armed workers, ordering everyone to sing Christmas carols.

Michael's coffin, in the room of the Old Man and Old Woman, is seen as the curtain goes up for the third act. A Man with Crutch, a Hunchback, a Woman with Withered Child, a Blind Man and a Young Man with Cough have come to pay their respects to the dead, to praise the church for the good things in life that are theirs and to condemn the strikers. Jack orders them away with the words: "Then go: go, you dead, and bury your dead: the living sleep here." The Red Priest enters and claims the body for the church; Julia and the Red Guards insist that his body belongs to the workers. The Red Priest orders his followers to carry the coffin to the church. Red Jim enters and together with his armed followers takes possession of the coffin. They exit and the cry: "Aha, Red Star, arise, the wide world over!" is heard as the procession marches away and the curtain falls.

The last act takes place in the lounge room in the residence of the Lord Mayor. Two Workmen, Joybell, the Old Man and the Lord Mayoress are busy preparing for the Christmas festivities in which the poor will be given some tea. Before the festivities can begin, sirens and pistol shots are heard announcing the outbreak of violence between the strikers and the police. Red Jim and the Red Guards enter the house and use it as a fortress. Barricades are set up in the streets as the battle rages. Jack is killed in the fighting, and Kian, when he discovers this, deserts the Saffron Shirts and comes over to the side of the workers. The Red Priest tries to prevail upon Red Jim to give up the fight; he urges the Brown Priest, who has joined the workers, to return to the church; and he entreats Kian to rejoin the Saffron Shirts. His requests are denied, and he leaves to the cry of, "Pass out the Red Priest of the politicians!" It is announced that the soldiers are joining the workers. "The Internationale" is heard in the distance as Red Jim tells Julia:

"You'll nurse, now, a far greater thing than a darling dead man. Up, young woman, and join in the glowing hour your lover died to fashion. He fought for life, for life is all; and death is nothing." (*Julia stands up with her right fist clenched. The playing and singing of "The Internationale" grow louder. Soldiers and sailors appear at the windows, and all join in the singing. The Red Star glows, and seems to grow bigger as the curtain falls.*)

From the above outline of the play it can be seen that O'Casey has forsaken the green of Irish national politics, the brown of the soldier's tunic, the gray of the Dublin slums, and the yellow of the primrose and has concentrated on the red of the Communists and the black of the Fascists. No other shades are permitted in this violent battle of ideologies and methodologies.

Clark and Freedley in their book, A *History of Modern Drama*, attempt to place O'Casey in respectable company rather than to evaluate the play for what it says and for what it stands. They claim that the play is not one in which communism is advocated:

"Some of O'Casey's greatest admirers either were baffled or annoyed by the implicit communism in *The Star Turns Red* (1940). Several readings of the play fail to bring to light any reason for such violent reactions on their part ... It is a fine and moving play which would scarcely seem more than left-liberal in production in the opinion of this writer."

Stephen Spender, on the other hand, claims that the play is straight "Party-Line" propaganda rather than a drama, and comes to the conclusion that the play must be bad because the Communists are shown as good. He further claims that O'Casey has "but a faltering hold on the implications of social ideas ... sympathises most with the Communist and understands best the Catholic."

George Jean Nathan, a long-time booster of O'Casey, states that "... the two worst influences on present-day playwrights are, very often, Strindberg and Communism ... Communism, one fears, has now adversely affected Sean O'Casey as a dramatic artist, as a perusal of his latest play, *The Star Turns Red*, disturbingly hints."

B. G. Brooks comments that "... when it was recently performed in London, *The Star Turns Red* gave many members of the audience a feeling that genius was being perverted for propagandist reasons, and that Mr. O'Casey, in his zeal for Communism had allowed his art to be sacrificed unforgivably."

The above few samples of critical comments on the play will suffice, perhaps, to give an idea of the reception that this play met at the hands of the critics. They reflect the opposition a play based on such material, presented in such a manner, is forced to overcome.

O'Casey knew he was dealing with a subject in such a way that he would again come up against an even more violent reaction this time than he did from the Dublin crowds with The Plough and the Stars, the Yeatsian type of criticism with The Silver Tassie, and the criticism reflected by James Agate with Within the Gates. Mention has previously been made of O'Casey's remark that he would not write to suit critics or government policy. The Star Turns Red flaunts his disregard of them both and is evidence of O'Casey's determination to write as he pleases.

Although O'Casey is primarily concerned with the struggle between the Right and the Left, he leaves the impression that he is also concerned with the problem of the individual and the mechanized mass, the forces driving man into conformity, and the exclusion of the middle way.

O'Casey's political portrait in this play reminds one of his military portrait in The Silver Tassie. Once again, he is concerned with the problem of man and the machine. In this case, The Star Turns Red, the political machine, replacing the military machine, swallows up the individual. It is not a question of good man or bad man, honest man or thief, but the question is which side are you on? The union leader, the church leader, the government official, the worker, the crippled, the aged—all must choose sides. O'Casey considers the decision to be an important one, a matter of life or death.

It is difficult to say whether we can equate O'Casey's sympathies in this play with the ideology of the Communist Party. Apparently, O'Casey sees in certain of the Communist ideals

84

an identity of interests with those of his own, but he does not seem to adhere, in a Marxian sense, to the Party Line. It is the Movement, not the Party, that is important. At no time is the Communist Party mentioned. It is a movement of the workers, and O'Casey does not clearly indicate party affiliations, if any. O'Casey has pictured modern political life with its Red Priest of the Right and its Brown Priest of the Left; its family of Communist Jacks and its Fascist Kians; its revolutionary Red Jims and its conservative union leaders; its hysterically religious Joybells and its ferociously militant Brannigans; its opportunistic Lord Mayors and its deterministic Julias.

When compared to *The Silver Tassie*, the lines of *The Star Turns Red* are different, the actors have changed their costumes, and the play is on a different stage. Yet, at the final curtain, the impression remains somewhat the same—people are but robots crushed down by mechanical forces. Organizations such as the trade unions, religious bodies such as the Red Priest's and Brown Priest's church, political bodies such as the Saffron Shirts and the Red Guards, family bodies such as the Old Man's, all of them are intricately tied together, inescapably bound in the life and death struggle for control of the state that is being waged by the Red and the Black.

O'Casey continued his drive toward the red horizon in his next play, *Red Roses for Me* (1943). In this play, however, the tone is more mild, the lines between worker and bourgeois are not so tightly drawn, the ideologies of communism and fascism are not presented in hard, uncompromising terms, and the characters themselves take on a more human aspect than the types in the previous play.

Perhaps one of the reasons for this more human approach

to many of the same problems raised in the previous play is the fact that here O'Casey went back to his own background and experiences for his material. We return, in a more definite way than in The Star Turns Red, to the Dublin slums and its inhabitants. The day-to-day lives of the people are presented as an integral part of the dramatic action. The hero of the play is, to a large extent, O'Casey himself; the minister is O'Casey's Protestant minister who was so sympathetically portrayed in his autobiography; in fact, many of the characters and incidents in the play can be found there.

The play is set during the time of the Transport Workers Strike of 1913, although O'Casey identifies the time of the play only as "a little while ago." Although we are again introduced to many of the same problems in this play as in The Star Turns Red, as has been mentioned, the human element that was lacking in the previous play now stands out so vividly that one critic claims that whereas O'Casey "clutched in dementia at school-boy Communism in The Star Turns Red, [he] has now passed on to the Apotheosis of Man, after the manner of Shelley, in Red Roses for Me."

The character of Ayamonn Breydon, a young Protestant worker of Dublin, eager for knowledge, absorbed in Shakespeare, active in the labor movement, disturbed by the conflicts between Catholicism and Protestantism, religion and atheism, in love with a Catholic girl, devoted to truth and beauty, is truly one of the great characters in all of O'Casey. He is the first male character in all of the plays who can take a place rightfully beside the great heroic woman, Juno Boyle. He has her warmth, her fortitude, her humanity, as well as other virtues that Juno did not have—a burning faith in mankind and a deep dynamic drive to bring to this earth in our time truth and justice. Ayamonn sacrifices, suffers and dies for his ideals just as Jack does in *The Star Turns Red*. However, death is enshrouded with his love for humanity; Jack's death is but a symbol of sacrifice for a cause. Ayamonn, like Prometheus, is willing to suffer as long as humanity gains thereby. *Red Roses for Me*, ennobled by this beautiful character, does indeed represent O'Casey's great love for the masses of the people; his desire to see a better life for the common man; and a reaffirmation that life must be realized through love as well as through wounds.

The strike is kept in the background and acts as merely that —background material against which the basic political and social problems are presented. Again, as in the previous play, we have workers battling police, religious tolerance struggling against religious bigotry, the living dead pitted against the dead living. The play ends, not with the waving of standards and the singing of revolutionary songs, but with the symbol of beauty and joy: "...deep in th' darkness a slim hand, so lovely, carries a rich bunch of red roses for me!"

The problem of a woman caught in the whirlpool of political and social strife in which she becomes bruised reoccurs in *Red Roses for Me*. Sheila, Ayamonn's sweetheart, tries to make him leave the ranks of the strikers by holding up before him the security and peace of the home and a comfortable marriage. Nora, as we remember, had a similar problem in *The Plough and the Stars*. She offered to her politically impassioned husband the warmth of her arms, the tenderness of her lips, and the comfort of the family hearth. Jack refused, and Nora, lonely and defeated, went mad. Yet, as we have pointed out, Nora emerged as a noble creature. Sheila, however, when Ayamonn refuses to give up his activities and is finally killed, emerges as a petty creature whose life revolves about her own petty desires. She becomes small and mean against the grandeur of Ayamonn's ideals and sacrifice. We even feel that, in spite of her refusal to go away with Ayamonn's murderer, Inspector Finglas, at the time of Ayamonn's death, it is not a refusal based on hatred for the destroyer of great ideals embodied in a great man, but a temporary emotional outburst resulting from loneliness.

Before we outline the plot of the play, a word must be said about the background material—the Transport Union Strike of 1913. This strike was no ordinary strike in which a handful of workers walked off their jobs in order to gain more pay. The Transport Strike was the most bitter battle between labor and capital in the history of Ireland and one of the most violent that has occurred in any country. The condition of the Dublin proletariat was such that a government board described it as "the worst in Europe." The Union, under the leadership of Jim Larkin, struck the transportation industry in the summer of 1913. The strike was marked by extreme violence almost from the beginning. The entire nation was rocked by the upheaval, and before long the church, the press, the government, and even certain labor officials were aligned against the strikers. The strikers, however, infuriated by the brutality of the police and the provocative actions of William Martin Murphy, described as an "arch strike-breaker...on whom the hatred of the proletariat was concentrated," refused to give in. The struggle lasted until 1914, when the workers finally went back to work. The strike had led to the formation of the Citizen Army, organized to protect the workers, and had drawn to it many individuals, like O'Casey, who were revolted by the brutality of the employers and the police. It convinced many people, including O'Casey, of the socialist thesis that the government was not a neutral body to preserve law and order but a weapon of force to be used, when necessary, against the proletariat.

This event and its results are reflected in O'Casey's play. Certain incidents of the strike are used; the general atmosphere of the struggle is re-created; and the fanatic idealism of the participating workers is portrayed. It is necessary to understand the strike in order to understand how Ayamonn, scholar, poet, worker, could become so involved in a cause that as a consequence of his belief he could say, "... this day's but a day's work done, an' it'll be begun again tomorrow." These were no idle words thrown into a hero's mouth by a partisan playwright; they were words pregnant with prophecy. Two years later, during Easter Week, the same men began their "work" again.

The play opens with Ayamonn, who lives with his mother in a two-room house in the Dublin slums, attempting to memorize Shakespeare's *King Henry VI* for a performance to raise money for workers' relief, while being constantly interrupted by Eeada, Dympna and Finnoola, three devout Catholic neighbor women, who are frantic over the apparent disappearance of their statue of the Lady of Eblana's poor; Sheila, his sweetheart, who wants him to leave his activities and devote his time to her; Brennan, a queer mixture of landlord and troubadour, who is always wondering if his money is safe in the Bank of Ireland; Roory O'Balacaun, a fervent Irish nationalist; and Mullcanny, an iconoclast. The result of all this interruption is that Shakespeare does not get memorized; the three women

89

are assured that all will be done to find their statue; Sheila does not succeed in convincing Ayamonn to drop his activities; Brennan is reassured for the hundredth time that the Bank of Ireland is a solid institution; Roory, the Irish Irelander, remains Roory, the Irish Irelander; and Mullcanny, unable to mock any more sacred things, leaves to seek greener fields.

In the first part of the second act, the characters and background of the period are further developed. Brennan, a Protestant, is revealed as a good-hearted fellow by his expenditure of money to clean up the grimy statue of the Queen of Eblana's poor. The shiny statue, anonymously returned to its owners, makes them very happy. The word goes around that a miracle has happened. The constant bickering between Protestant and Catholic and loyalist and Republican is exemplified in the argument between Brennan, loyalist and Protestant, and Roory, Republican and Catholic. Brennan sums up one viewpoint when he says, "...God save th' King, an' tae hull with th' Pope!" Roory presents the other side when he shouts, "...to hell with th' King an' God save th' Pope!" Ayamonn's viewpoint on freedom is made clear when he says:

"Let us bring freedom here, not with sounding brass an' tinkling cymbal, but with silver trumpets blowing, with a song all men can sing, with a palm branch in our hand, rather than with a whip at our belt, and a headsman's axe on our shoulders."

His place, he feels, is with the workers, and he is willing to sacrifice Sheila's love rather than desert them. When Sheila urges him to put his own advancement ahead of his concern for other people and desert the strike, he answers:

"D'ye know what you're asking me to do, woman? To be a black-leg; to blast with th' black frost of desertion the gay hopes

90

of my comrades. Whatever you may think them to be, they
are my comrades. Whatever they may say or do, they remain
my brothers and sisters. Go to hell, girl. I have a soul to save
as well as you."

To express his sympathy with the strikers, he agrees to speak
at their meeting, even though the Rector has brought him a
warning that violence will be used against the men and that
Ayamonn's life is in danger. When Sheila urges the Rector
to forbid Ayamonn to go to the meeting, saying that God is
against it, the Rector replies: "Who am I to say that God's
against it? You are too young by a thousand years to know
the mind of God. If they be his brothers, he does well among
them." The act ends with singing before the Statue of the
Queen of Eblana's poor by the men and women of the
tenement:

> "Oh, Queen of Eblana's poor children
> Bear swiftly our woe away,
> An' give us a chance to live lightly,
> An hour of our life's dark day!"

The third act takes place in a Dublin street by a bridge that
crosses the river Liffey. Three specimens of Dublin misery,
Eeada, Dympna and Finnoola, are seen hawking their wares.
The abject poverty and suffering of the slum-dwellers are vividly
portrayed. Brennan, who insists upon singing a merry tune to
the wretched individuals, is told by one of them to "go away
an' leave us to saunter in sleep, an' crave out a crust in the grey
kingdom of quietness." Ayamonn enters and tells them of his
vision of a gay life, free from suffering. The stage grows brighter,
and the faces of the desolate poor lose their mark of death.

In a frenzy of joy, the people dance and sing as the vision of a new beautiful Dublin is unfolded to them by Ayamonn. The city and the people become transfigured. However, the march of soldiers' feet on the way to the meeting of the strikers returns them to reality. The act closes with the people singing quietly:

> "We swear to release thee from hunger and hardship,
> From things that are ugly and common and mean;
> The people together shall build a great city,
> The finest and fairest that ever was seen."

The last act opens on the grounds of the Protestant church of St. Burnupus. The Rector, desirous of giving a touch of joy to his church, has decorated it with some primroses. He is roundly condemned as a Papist by Foster and Dowzard, two stalwarts of the church. Sheila again tries to prevent Ayamonn from going to the meeting, but is rebuffed. The Inspector warns him that "...the people of power today will teach a lesson many will remember for ever; though some fools may not live long enough to learn it." His mother, unable to prevail upon him to stay away from the meeting, sends him off with the words: "Go on your way, my son, an' win. We'll welcome another inch of the world's welfare." Ayamonn leaves. Workers enter and throw stones and insults at Foster and Dowzard, who have been scabbing in the strike. Shortly thereafter men and women rush into the church grounds to escape from the police, who have opened fire upon the workers. Word reaches the church that Ayamonn has been killed. His body is brought to the church. The Rector, in answer to Mrs. Breydon's complaint that her son is now lonesome, replies: "He's not so lonesome as you think, dear friend, but alive and laughing in the midst of God's gay welcome." The play ends with Brennan softly singing:

> "A sober, black shawl hides her body entirely,
> Touch'd be th' sun an' th' salt spray of th' sea;
> But deep in th' darkness a slim hand, so lovely,
> Carries a rich bunch of red roses for me!"

Red Roses for Me, in addition to being an expression of O'Casey's political and social idealism, is the most complete presentation of his ideas on Ireland and its problems. The plays of his "Irish War Period," for all of their dramatic intensity and description of social and political problems, were plays that offered no hope, no ultimate aims, no solutions. The two decades or so that had intervened between the trio of early plays and Red Roses for Me had matured O'Casey to the point of insisting that a horizon as well as a landscape be drawn of society. Red Roses for Me, unlike The Star Turns Red, does not present the exact solution or preach violently for the attainment of that solution: it gives a picture of the present and a vision of the future.

We must understand Ireland, with its conflicts in government and religion, to understand clearly the problems of the drama. Contradictions of all kinds present themselves to us in the history of Ireland, and these are reflected in the contradictory characters in this play. Brennan, a Protestant, spends his carefully hoarded money to repaint a statue of a Catholic saint; Roory, a hater of anything foreign, condemns the King of England and praises the Pope of Rome; Eeada, Dympna and Finnoola lose their treasured statue and turn to the Protestant, Ayamonn, to find it for them; Mrs. Breydon, possessed of a

93

deep love for her son, blesses the cause that she feels will bring death to him; Ayamonn, desirous of bringing freedom to the land in a peaceful manner, participates willingly in violent events.

It is these contradictions brought into the glare of the sunlight that make O'Casey's play such a penetrating picture of Ireland, its people, and its problems. And when he adds to this picture a vision of hope on the horizon, red though it may be, his play ceases to be only a picture of an Ireland of bygone days but becomes also a prophecy of what he believes the future may well hold in store for the grandchildren of Cathleen ni Hoolihan.

seven

THE WORLD AT WAR AND AFTER

The struggle against Nazi conquest during World War II brought together classes and countries whose basic interests and ideologies were not identical, but whose need for self-preservation against a common enemy made them working allies, at least until the danger had passed. Employee and employer sat around the table and discussed how to increase war production; master and servant joined air raid organizations; Communist and conservative fought together on the battlefield; collectivistic Russia and individualistic Britain and the United States formed an alliance. The danger of a common enemy submerged, for the time, animosities and differences. It is this temporary reconciliation of opposites that forms the political background of O'Casey's play on World War II, *Oak Leaves and Lavender* (1946).

Life is a dangerous game in time of war; the scent of lavender is always near, and death unconcernedly takes both the "prince and the prick-louse." War is a sharpening of the violence that is all about us; security of person is an illusion; struggle is the staff of life. Wounds must be the result of sacrifice, and sacrifice itself places man close to God. The living

95

must squeeze the last ounce of joy from life: the joy of man and woman beautifully united as one; the joy of planting acorns from which sturdy oaks will grow; the joy of free men defending their freedom against the death-hand of slavery. All this O'Casey tells us in his drama about the people of Britain during the dark days of England's battle against the Nazis.

The play opens with a prelude. In a large manorial house the ancestral shades of the manor's great past dance to the music of a minuet. They are frightened because their peace has been disturbed; they are fretful lest the torches of freedom that they kept lit will be forever extinguished now that the flame of liberty is in the hands of the mass of people. They dolefully pass out of sight as the voice of the seller of lavender is heard singing in a mournful voice.

The action of the drama centers around the manor of Dame Hatherleigh, a woman of aristocratic background, during the Battle of Britain. War-time activity and atmosphere are re-created, we are introduced to blackout curtains, air raid wardens, official regulations, conservation programs, military inductions, air raids, etc.

In this atmosphere, Feelim O'Morrigun, the Irish butler, humorously reflects the harassment and difficulties of war activities on the home front. Dame Hatherleigh's son, Edgar, a likable youth of the upper classes, and Feelim's son, Drishogue, a Communist, are close friends. They are waiting, as the play opens, for assignment to active duty in the air force, having recently completed their training. Monica, a farmer's daughter, and Jennie, a volunteer land worker, go the limit to make the last few days of non-active duty that the boys have days of pleasure and delight. Abraham Penryhn, Monica's father, sees nothing but evil in his daughter's affair with Drishogue, but is unable to prevent it. Dame Hatherleigh is opposed to Edgar's affair with Jennie, but with characteristic upper class good breeding offers no obvious interference.

Through the characters of Pobjoy, a conscientious objector, Mr. Constant, a man eager to flee to America, and Mrs. Deeda Tutting, a sympathizer with fascism and a bitter anti-Communist, we are introduced to discussions on pacifism, patriotism and political ideologies. Drishogue presents the Communist viewpoint, Feelim the Irish, and Dame Hatherleigh the conservative British.

The boys leave for the front, and the scent of lavender, the odor of death, present from time to time since the beginning of the play, becomes more noticeable. Tragedy descends quickly upon the Hatherleigh household. Both boys are killed in action. Jennie dies, also, trying to rescue Edgar, her lover, from his burning plane. Monica, left behind with the seed of Drishogue within her, bravely cries: "There's more to come; a living spark from himself that will soon be a buoyant symbol of our Drishogue who is gone!"

Feelim vows to stand by her even though he feels that "the gettin' o' children should be done accordin' to rule!" Dame Hatherleigh, overcome by the loss of her only son, tonelessly remarks: "We must all go soon. Our end makes but a beginning for others."

The shadowy dancers enter the room and Dame Hatherleigh tells them that she will join them as soon as she finds her son. She sinks to the floor as the voice of the Lavender Seller is heard chanting her wares outside the window:

97

"Ladies, buy my bonnie lavender,
Incense for your snowy sheetings,
Giving charm to all ruling joys
Measur'd out in lovers' meetings!
Lavender, lavender,
Ladies, buy my bonnie laven-lavender!"

Although O'Casey's sympathy was on the side of Britain in World War II, it was a sympathy that was dictated by his hatred for fascism rather than an uncritical love for England. He was willing to support to the fullest Britain's efforts to preserve her freedom and the cultural and scientific achievements of her great men from the threat of Nazi destruction, but his ultimate aims were not the preservation of the British Empire or the present social structure of England. He, too, formed a temporary alliance with the very political and social system that he desired to see changed. O'Casey's viewpoint is clearly expressed by Drishogue when the playwright has the Irish lad answer Edgar's question in the following scene:

EDGAR. Which England? There are so many of them: Conservative England, Liberal England, Labour England, and your own Communist England—for which of them shall I go forth to fight, and perchance, to die?

DRISHOGUE. For all of them in the greatness of England's mighty human soul set forth in what Shakespeare, Shelley, Keats, and Milton sang; in the mighty compass of Darwin's mind . . . for what your Faraday did in taming the lightning . . . Go forth to fight, perchance to die, for the great human soul of England. Go forth to fight and to destroy, not the enemies of this or that belief, but the enemies of mankind. In this fight, Edgar, right-

98

eousness and war have kissed each other: Christ, Mahomet, Confucius, and Buddha are one.

O'Casey further clarifies his position in the following scene between Drishogue and Monica:

> MONICA. . . . I sometimes wish you hadn't ventured into danger for the love of England!
>
> DRISHOGUE. Love of England! Good God, woman, I have no love for England!
>
> MONICA. But aren't you fighting for her?
>
> DRISHOGUE. No, I'm not! I'm fighting for the people. I'm fighting against the stormy pillagers who blackened the time-old walls of Guernica, and tore them down ...

O'Casey has a great deal of admiration for the bravery of the English people. His characters, with but a few exceptions, exemplify courage under fire, steadfastness of purpose and moral fortitude. Rich and poor alike are presented as submerging their personal concern for the safety of all. It is an elaborate picture of heroism under the most difficult of circumstances. There is no despair and no shirking. Danger is met full-face, and impending death does not scar the full-flush of vibrant life vigorously lived.

One critic views this aspect of the play in the following way: "Heroism has come back to the earth—this time in England —and the energy of all Britain is mobilized to fight off the invader of her skies. The young seek to drain life quickly in each other's arms; the old seek consolation for the death of both young and old in the reflection that birth goes on in the midst of death, the curlew calls, the plovers cry, and new oaks 'strut from dying acorns.'"

The conscientious objector, Pobjoy, is scornfully treated.

His protestation that he hates war and violence is brushed aside as the sentiments of a coward. O'Casey's treatment of Pobjoy is a far cry from his own pacifist sentiments so forcefully presented in The Silver Tassie. His concern over the loss of even one life sacrificed for a cause, so dramatically outlined in the plays of his "Irish War Period," is not to be found in this play. Now pacifism means surrender to slavery, and the loss of life for some assures the continuation of life for many.

The Mosley-type British Fascist, Mrs. Deeda Tutting, is portrayed as a hysterical, bigoted fanatic. Her Russophobia is matched only by her admiration of Germany and her contempt for democracy. She repeats, parrot-like, all the arguments in the book against the Godless and ruthless Communists and the bloated and degenerate democracies. She feels that the National Socialists have been mistreated and misunderstood. One example will suffice, perhaps, to give a picture of Mrs. Deeda Tutting's type of thinking:

"I tell you, young man, the National Socialism of Germany, in many respects, is far superior to Soviet Rule; and if it only gives up its racial animosity, and its spirit of conquest, its Germany will become more cultured than even Britain's or France's pompous and hypocritical imperialism!"

Drishogue, the Communist, is portrayed as a sincere, clever lad, the finest that Erin could produce. His speeches defending the Soviet Union very often sound like an editorial from a Communist newspaper or an order of the day from the Soviet High Command. His Irish eloquence places his remarks on a higher level than the frantic outbursts of Mrs. Tutting, but the eloquence does not fully cover the editorializing. One of his editorial speeches, for instance, is the following: "Woe unto

100

any nation making war on the Soviet Union! She will slash open the snout, and tear out the guts of any power crossing her borders!" A few moments later, however, this tone is dropped and Drishogue slips into Irish eloquence:

"Over in the east, the people took their first fine step forward, and they look over the rim of the world now. Many can see them clearly, and many more can hear them cheering. We know full well the hardships before us. Our spring will still have many a frosty morning and a frosty night; our summers hot hold many a burden for us; our autumn glory will still be tinged with many a starless night, the sound of sorrow loud beneath their shrouded silence; but winter's night of hopeless woe is gone forever, and the people's energetic joy shall sound like well-cast bells through every passing season!"

Through Drishogue, we realize that O'Casey's red horizon is still there, a red horizon toward which he would have the people of the entire world march.

In *Cock-a-doodle Dandy* (1949), he returns once again to Irish rural settings and characters. Although O'Casey does not definitely set the time of the play, it is safe to assume that it takes place in contemporary Ireland.

Nine years previously, O'Casey wrote about rural Ireland in *Purple Dust*, and in that play certain nostalgic traces could be found for the land where he spent the first forty years or so of his life. But in *Cock-a-doodle Dandy* even these traces are missing.

O'Casey now breaks with Ireland completely. He has no faith in her ability to loosen the heavy hand of the clergy which has narrowed the vision and life of her people. Those individuals who wish to lead the joyful life must escape to other lands, just as certain characters in the play, Loreleen, Lorna, Marion, The Messenger (and O'Casey himself) did. It is as though, for the time being at least, O'Casey admits that the church-state, which he considers Ireland to be, is too powerful to be beaten and too stubborn to be changed. After almost a quarter of a century in exile, O'Casey, undoubtedly, sees no amelioration of the narrow, confining and unenlightened conditions which forced him to emigrate. And in anger and grief, he hurls another lightning bolt of criticism at the land he loves so dearly. For although the play is lively and full of fun, there is a Pagliaccian motif throughout. O'Casey laughs, but he cannot hide his tears. His first love was Cathleen ni Houlihan, and scourge her as he will, he is faithful to her in his fashion.

The play, a capricious mixture of fantasy and realism, takes place in an Irish rural area. It opens with Michael Marthraun, "a small farmer, now the owner of a lucrative bog," which he has purchased from his second wife's father for fifty pounds, and Sailor Mahan, "once a sailor, now the owner of a fleet of lorries carrying turf from bog to town," haggling over the price for Sailor Mahan's services.

But very soon it becomes obvious that there are sinister and evil forces at work in Nyadnanave. An audacious rooster, symbol of proud, vibrant living, the dawn of a new day, the very rhythm of universal life, a cynical mocker of those human beings who would shy away from life and bury themselves in the dark and gloomy recesses of ignorance and superstition, parades, flutters and crashes his way through the Marthraun household and the adjacent neighborhood. His jauntiness is matched by Loreleen, pretty daughter of Michael Marthraun by his first wife, who lives for love and loves to live, embracing in her fair arms all the gaiety, warmth and understanding that life has to offer.

Michael fears that gay Loreleen, who has but recently come back to Ireland from England, is bedeviling his household and is the cause of "sinisther signs appearin' everywhere," because of her free and easy ways. His second wife, Lorna, and Marion, a servant in his house, also creatures who would rather delight in dance and song than darken their lives by following the gloomy directives of Father Domineer, the parish priest, and The Messenger, Marion's lover, look on disapprovingly and unbelievingly as Michael, Mahan, Father Domineer, Shanaar, a mouther of Latin and bearer of superstitious tales, One-Eyed Larry, "a peasant lad and potential sacristan" and the Sergeant, a Civic Guard, tremble, plot, fume and fight their fantastic battles against the irrepressible cock, devils in whiskey bottles and flying top hats.

The realistic mingles freely with the supernatural: poor Julia, Lorna's sister and a victim of paralysis, sets off with her father for Lourdes, hoping to be the recipient of a miracle, and returns later with the mark of death plainly written on her face; Father Domineer, in a fit of anger against a Lorry Driver who is living out of wedlock with a woman, strikes him down, accidentally killing him, and murmuring "an act of contrition into th' poor man's ear" dispatches him, purified, to his Maker; Mahan, firm-believer, offers Loreleen five pounds so that she will have enough money to "weigh anchor, an' be off outa this damned place" if she will allow herself "to be ruffled a bit."

The denouement comes with a disheveled and bruised Loreleen being dragged into the garden of Michael's house, having been discovered making love with a respectable married man, Sailor Mahan. Father Domineer, at the head of the pack, abuses her for her immorality and orders her banished so that she'll "dhribble th' blackness of sin no longer over our virtuous bordhers!"

Loreleen leaves with Lorna accompanying her into exile. Lorna cries: "... we're free from th' Priest an' his rabble. Lift up your heart, lass: we go, not towards an evil, but leave an evil behind us!"

Father Domineer tells Michael not to fret that his wife has left him, for "th' demon is conquered—you can live peaceful an' happy in your own home now." Michael, disconsolate, does not ask Father Domineer but The Messenger what he should do. The Messenger replies: "Die. There is little else left useful for the likes of you to do."

The Messenger, accompanied by Marion, goes to join Loreleen and Lorna in exile, stating that he is going "to a place where life resembles life more than it does here." He sings a merry song about his loved one, Marion, as he departs, but old Michael, left alone in a lonely and forsaken house, "leans forward on the table, and buries his head in his arms."

In comparison with his last play about contemporary Ireland, *Purple Dust*, the characters who people this play are by far less forward-looking. Bosses and workers alike are fear-filled, tied inescapably to the church and its doctrines. There are no shrewd and sharp proletarians filled with native wit and keenness, but instead there are sheep-like men who prate with the prattlers and hurl abuse at all who do not hew to the line of prescribed living. There are no O'Killigains ripping away the veil of paternal imperialism from the British or enlightened workers fierce in their pride for what ancient Ireland contributed to world culture, but instead the O'Killigains have all become narrow-fisted, self-seeking, superstition-soaked, petty entrepreneurs like Michael Marthraun and Sailor Mahan, exploiting their workers, unconcerned with the glory and promise of Ireland, tied hand and foot to the most backward and ignorant dogmas, and the workers have all become Rough Fellows, creatures who run with the pack, vicious and dogma-dulled, ready to cast the first stone at a wayward young girl: a far cry from the workers in *Purple Dust*, lively lovers of life, who audaciously run away with the bored mistresses of rich Englishmen!

As in many of his previous plays, it is the men who are unenlightened, bogged down with superstition and religiosity which darken the day and bring on an eternal night, slaves to material pursuits that chase away all laughter from their souls, narrowing their lives and keeping them from merry ways that could brighten this earth. Every male character in the play, with the exception of The Messenger, is of this stamp. It is the women, again, who are the hope and the light, brave, bright, youthful souls who face life head-on, giving free reign to love and love's delights. This is true for every woman in the play, with the possible exception of poor, dying Julia, and even she, paralytic that she is, is willing to travel far, seeking for a miracle to cure her rather than wait patiently, resignedly for death.

The church, exemplified by Father Domineer, is scourged for its insistence on gloom instead of glow, its preoccupation with driving out of the hearts of humanity the joy of the dance, the delight of the song, the gaiety of love and passion. O'Casey pictures the church as stubbornly medieval in its belief in the supernatural, ignorantly intolerant of the fierce fire that attracts the opposite sexes, wretchedly wrapped up in ritual and dogma, unalterably opposed to man's artistic creations which might move people into the sunstreams of joyful contemplation of widening horizons and away from the mesmerizing influences of uncomprehended Latin chants.

As he did in *Within the Gates*, O'Casey calls for a church of joy and laughter instead of a church of sorrow and penance. Who is Loreleen if not the Young Whore of *Within the Gates*, that same Young Whore who insists that she'll "die dancing?" Who is The Messenger if not The Dreamer in that same play who would leave behind all dirge-songs and envelop himself and all those about him with uplifting lilting refrains, honoring the joy that is to be had in the life lived lively? It is as though, after sixteen years, O'Casey felt compelled to reaffirm his distaste for merchants of gloom, and the need to present once again to a world which is so weighed down with evil, sorrow, hate and fear a call to present arms in the cause of laughter and a full, ripe, undeceitful, youthful and joyful life revolving about the open, unashamed, vibrant love of man for woman and woman for man.

The fairy-story element in the play, the light fantasy that humorously brightens up the action, the slapstick that tickles and the Joxerian dialogue that amuses, all contribute to make *Cock-a-doodle Dandy* a hilariously funny piece. Yet, shot full of low comedy and the laugh of life as it is, it contains a prophetic dirge-note of the day to come when the piously stupid

106

and the stupidly pious who have a leer on their lips instead of a lilt in their throats will be no more.

It is no accident that O'Casey has a sweep-clean wind raging throughout the last scene of the play, throwing wild consternation into the hearts of the Sergeant of the Civic Guard, One-Eyed Larry, the Bellman, a crier of superstitious nonsense, and Michael Marthraun, faithful to his priest, but unfaithful to his own flesh; yet, this same wind holds no terror for The Messenger, Lorna or Marion. It is also not an accident that the flag-pole upon which the Irish Tricolour flies so proudly is blown down when the wind rages. O'Casey does not forget the "state" in the church-state that he condemns.

Cock-a-doodle Dandy, for all of its whimsical humor, ingenious fantasy and zany slapstick, is a burning indictment of Irish puritanism, and is chock-full of political and social satire; it is a call for man to live the full life replete with love and understanding.

eight

THE LAST HURRAHS

"Here, with whitened hair, desires failing, strength ebbing out of him, with the sun gone down, and with only the serenity and calm warning of the evening star left to him, he drank to Life, to all it had been, to what it was, to what it would be. Hurrah!"

Thus, O'Casey described himself in his autobiography at the beginning of the last decade of his life—about the same time he was to undertake his last two full-length plays, *The Bishop's Bonfire* and, subsequently, *The Drums of Father Ned*.

Here again, as in his immediately previous play, *Cock-a-doodle Dandy*, O'Casey returns to the country from which he exiled himself for his setting, his characters, his themes—and his full-throated, anger-through-tears-and-laughter criticisms and laments of Ireland. Brutally and boisterously, laughingly and liltingly, he examines the people and the institutions.

Sometimes with a dirgelike repetitiveness and sometimes by hurling verbal thunderbolts, O'Casey chants or bellows familiar political and social themes that he had devoted his entire life to exposing: political fraud, nationalist hypocrisy, sensual puritanism, blind obedience to authority, the dulling gloom of a dogmatic church, and the shallow thoughts and cold, restraining hand of middle-class morality.

And sometimes with a merry tune and a naive faith in the human being and the promise of beauty and glory in the human condition, he sings poignantly—and, too often, pratlingly—of an unsophisticated, uncosmopolitan, un-atomic age, Utopian desires and dreams: the worth of the individual, the promise of the future, the glorious trinity of hope, beauty, and dignity, and, in general, man's unquenchable thirst for a full, free life.

To the very end of his long life (he died at 84) and to the very last play he wrote, *The Drums of Father Ned*, he firmly refused to be a cynical negativist, a disgruntled critic of the social order, or a callous iconoclast. He remained to his last breath and to the last word of the last scene of his last play an unconquerable optimist. As O'Casey himself noted, his works and his life with their sharp criticisms and arguments had made him "tattered and torn, like a man tossed by the cow with the crumpled horn, but still sparring for defense and a forward blow."

It is indeed true that O'Casey never gave up or gave in, despite poor health for most of his life, a bitter lack of commercial success with his plays that resulted in almost continuous financial difficulties, and personal tragedies such as the death of his young son and near-blindness for a good part of his later life. Of this period, the critic Brooks Atkinson, who visited him at his home, wrote:

"If it had not been for his unconquerable spirit, the last years in his third-story flat in Torquay, Devon, might have been dismal. He had very little physical strength; he could no longer read the books that surrounded him or enjoy the pictures in his hallways. But it was a stimulating experience to visit him. The sincerity of his convictions, the humor of his conversation, the wide range of his knowledge gave an impression of great spiritual vitality. A darlin' man, as Joxer said in *Juno and the Paycock*."

It is precisely this "spiritual vitality" that shines through his last two plays and which covers over their many faults when they are examined in the full panoply of O'Casey's life work. For these plays say little that O'Casey has not said before— and, oftentime, much better. As it will be seen in an examination of the plays that follow, what the plays reveal is a thematically tired old playwright. Sad, sad. Yet, if O'Casey has little that is new to tell us, nevertheless, as old people sometimes do, he insists upon telling us over and over of his observations and his philosophy with the hope that a lesson may be learned, a viewpoint changed, a heart uplifted, a human being redeemed—and a world made clean, pure, joyful, and cozy warm.

The Bishop's Bonfire opens in the home and garden of the pompous-ass Councillor Reiligan, where a few villagers are at work improving the house for the return visit of Bishop Mullarky to his native village. In short order, we are introduced to a group of characters that O'Casey fans have met before. Here is the hypocritically pious villager, Rankin by name, who, as O'Casey describes him, is "obsessed with a sense of ever-present sin and his nostrils frequently sniffing the fogs of hell." Another villager, the Prodical, is "sour and pugnacious," and the third is the inevitable counter-character, a Daniel Clooncoohy, who is "young, twenty-five or so, and good-looking

111

in a rugged way" with an "open and innocent" face. The "dreamer" type is introduced as Manus Moanroe. The good, forward-looking churchman is Father Boheroe, the curate; and the bad, backward-looking churchman is Canon Burren, the parish priest of the village of Ballyoonagh. The sly, wise, free-spirited character is the 84-year-old Codger, who "carries his age about with him in a jaunty and defiant way" and in many ways reminds one of O'Casey himself. The male cast is rounded out by Reiligan's son Michael.

The female characters are only two in number, both of them Councillor Reiligan's daughters. Keelin, the forward-looking girl, is "a handsome lass of 25 ... her hair is a ripe auburn ... her figure is slim, though her breasts be buxom." Foorawn, the backward-looking daughter, is two years older than her sister. She tries to give her "fair face a look of resolute and austere serenity," and men lift their hats "respectfully in tribute to her reputation of piety and in reverence for the vow of perpetual chastity with which she has burdened herself."

Rankin and the Prodical constantly bicker about who is doing the most work, and complain about Daniel who would rather not work on the house but would rather breeze with Manus about "building our temples higher and higher till the shouting of heavenly pride encases and hides the growling-grumble of men," and spoon with his loved one, Keelin. Keelin, on her part, teases the pious Rankin by insisting he take a lip-smacking look at her leg as she lifts up her skirt, and when he literally spits in her face for taunting him, she cries in an outburst reminiscent of the Young Whore's magnificent speech to the Bishop in *Within the Gates*:

"You dirty, evil-minded lugworm! You huckster of hollow

112

an' spiteful holiness! You get! Looka the fella who wants to be great with God! Christ, you'll make a commotion when you get, you get, to where you're goin'! Crawlin' to heaven the way the snake crawled outa Eden! Damn you, you God's remorse for men!"

Father Boheroe tries to spread good cheer to the men by assuring them that "work, too, is holy, but only when it's reasonable." The Prodical speaks about the great day that is coming when they will all build a bonfire "to light a welcome to the comin' Bishop, an' piles of bad books an' evil pictures on top of it are to go away in flames." And Rankin completes the stacking of the deck as well as the bonfire by saying: "Pitch them in, all in—bad pictures, bad books—pitch them into the burnin' bonfire!"

The Canon enters and is soon chastising the Codger for his "mischievous old mouth," and Father Boheroe for his liberality. Manus attempts to tell Foorawn of his love for her, but she tells him she has pledged herself to God, that he speaks blasphemously, and is a "bad man." The act ends with Codger and Daniel—the believers in joy—planning to go to the meadow to listen to "the lark singin' in the clear air."

The second act takes place in the drawing room of Councillor Reiligan's house. In quick succession, we are re-introduced to Rankin's hypocritical piety, Reiligan's pomposity, the Codger's irreverence, and Daniel's mixture of iconoclasm, patriotism, and personal weakness. Michael's flag-waving patriotism and bombast ring out loudly and ludicrously: "You see, men, Ireland's so important, geographically, that, in a war, the Russians would need to take her over within an hour, within an hour."

The play hangs on dead center as one favorite O'Casey subject after another is disposed of against the background of talk on the Bishop's impending visit—from the fear of Bolsheviks "flutterin' down from the Irish skies on to our emerald sod" to the heavy hand of the Church—"What are we doin' but weavin' a way through life, content with an odd prayer to propel us towards where none of us wants to go!"

Toward the end of the act, Keelin is distressed to discover that Daniel, her lover, is too weak to stand up for his love for her in the face of opposition to the rich girl-poor boy marriage. In desperation, she cries to the good Father Boheroe who has championed their cause, "What am I to do, Father ... Dan hadn't the courage to stand up to them. Dan has forsaken me, forsaken me!" And after the good Father comforts her—"My poor child!"—she asks him: "What was that, Father? A shiver cold and powerful through my body into my soul." The curtain falls as the good Father replies: "It was, my child, a long, sad sigh from God."

In the third, and last, act, Keelin refuses to be given in marriage to a fifty-year-old man by the Canon and her father; the Codger is banished from the Councillor's employ because of his irreverence; Manus shakes the sod of Ireland from his feet, the love of Foorawn from his heart, and plans to go to England; Father Boheroe, upon seeing love unrequited and the dismal ways of bigoted people, says bravely in a cry that could be O'Casey's own:

"It is easy to turn one's back on things, but it is better and braver to face them. I shall never turn my back on a beautiful world, nor on the beautiful flesh of humanity, asparkle with vigour, intelligence, and health."

The play ends with the announced arrival of the Bishop and the lighting of the Bishop's bonfire. The forward-looking characters do not attend—Manus, Father Boheroe, and the Codger. In fact, the Codger and the Prodical go off to get drunk, and just as the Irish swilled in *The Plough and the Stars* as Ireland was fighting for her freedom to have her own state, the Irish swill during a celebration glorifying a leader of their Church.

The play ends with the Prodical saying impatiently: "Never mind about the lantern, the Bishop, or the Bishop's Bonfire—them's trivial things!" He and the Codger sing a song, Manus leaves for a brighter, more joyous land, and proclaiming the persistent, undefeated-as-yet power of the Church, the Bishop's bonfire "flames higher and more brightly" as the play ends.

The Drums of Father Ned, also set in Ireland, is a variation on the same theme as O'Casey's previous two plays; namely, man has another nature—the joyous life, the pleasures of love, the song of work and family and comradeship on the one hand as opposed to the drabness of religiosity, the stupidity of class superiority, and the dreariness of the moralistic life on the other hand.

The play, in sum, deals with the fear that the established, well-off citizens have in the face of a changing world, even a changing attitude toward life. The setting is the Tostal Festival, supported and cheered by the young and by a joyful, exuberant spirit symbolized by a Father Ned, who is talked about but never appears.

At the end of the play, O'Casey, through one of his characters, cries: "Lasses an' lads, it's time to go, for more life, more laughter; a sturdier spirit and a stronger heart. Father Ned is on the march!"

The Drums of Father Ned was not produced as it was scheduled to be in 1958 at the Tostal Festival, together with a play by James Joyce, which was rejected, and a play by Samuel Beckett, which he withdrew. For his part, O'Casey refused to make certain alterations in his play that were requested by the Roman Catholic Archbishop of Dublin, and the Festival collapsed. Later, in 1959, the play had its world premiere in the United States, by the Little Theatre Group, in Lafayette, Indiana.

There is little doubt that these last two plays of O'Casey, these "last hurrahs," are dramatically weak and thematically repetitive. It is as though O'Casey in the twilight of his life had a compulsion to sum up all he resolutely—and stubbornly —stood for all his life, so that there would be no misunderstanding that here was one Irishman who did not bend his knee to any of the accepted powers of this earth—the state, the church, middle-class morality, the "successful" life, the demonic drive for money, and acceptability by the so-called established order.

It is not surprising that O'Casey's last plays are set in Ireland. For O'Casey, for all of his world outlook in his later years, his anarchistic, undisciplined brand of communistic belief, and his long love affair with the Soviet Union, returned in his last years to his first and greatest and truest love— Ireland. In his last years, O'Casey wrote with all the passion at his command:

"I know the mind of Ireland because I am within it; I know the heart of Ireland because I am one of its corners; I know the five senses of Ireland because I am within them and they are within me; they bid me look, and when I look, I

116

see; they bid me listen, and when I listen, I hear. Tell us what you see, says Ireland, and tell us what you hear; you speak out, son, and break the silence; for so many of the others are so afraid of their damned souls that they can but mutter prayers no good to God."

Yet, O'Casey is no "professional" Irishman. His vision is too broad, his understanding of people too mellow, his joy of life too unrestrained to be bound inescapably by the confines of one country. And again and again O'Casey beseeches, teases, cajoles, threatens, and tickles us to "laugh, and be proud to belong to the old proud pageant of man."

So it is, then, that these two last plays, together with *Cock-a-doodle Dandy* with which they must be considered for an understanding of O'Casey's last phase, are a further expression of O'Casey's philosophy of life—a philosophy based upon the dignity of man and the joy that can be had in the free life, unrestricted by blind prejudice, religious superstition, political chicanery, and human stupidity. They are the last of a long line of bitterly truthful dramas—plays that will stand for many years as a portrait of an age.